LA GAMBA

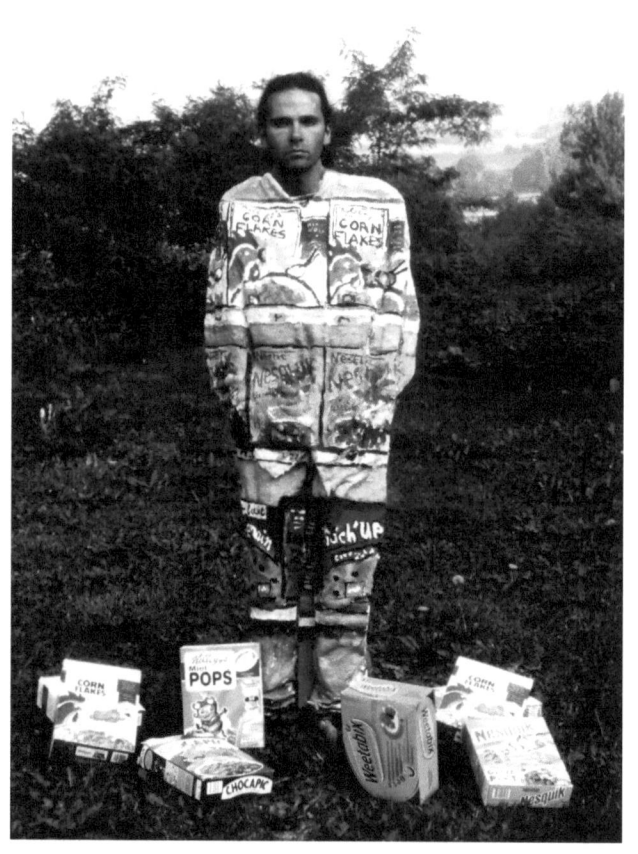

(Laurent La Gamba outside his studio,
in Monléon-Magnoac, France, Mai 2001)

Laurent
La Gamba

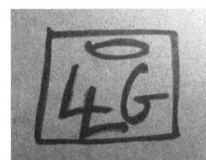

Cover: *Skip*, 2002 Pro-cryptic painting (acrylic on board and protective suit) color photograph, 75 x 50 cm

Back cover: *Open fridge*, 2002 Pro-cryptic painting (acrylic on board and protective suit) color photograph, 75 x 50 cm

Laurent La Gamba

The art of camouflage

Texts and illustrations collected by Claire Duane

Matisse Matisse Av 4100 *Avenue Books*

ISBN: 9781500655211

Contents

Laurent La Gamba
The art of camouflage

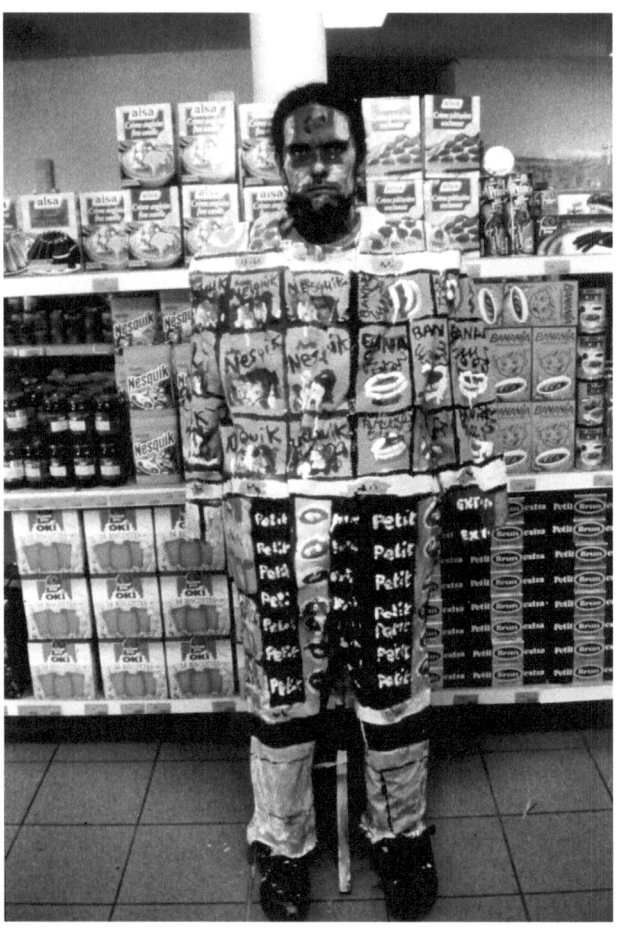

Petits Brun Extra, Self-portrait, 2002 Pro-cryptic painting (acrylic on board and protective suit) color photograph, 75 x 50 cm

Foreword

" It appears Mr. La Gamba doesn't want to be seen.

However, a closer look reveals his face, sculptured into everyday miscellany. The rest of him…well, that's another story. Dubbed Procrypsis by the artist, his self-instigated phenomenon has gained him worldwide recognition. Within the clutter of confined urban environments, this innovative Frenchman weaves himself into the scene, leaving little human trace. It only seems that the space itself has taken on a new, interesting shape.

In exploring the fundaments of camouflage, La Gamba reveals a means of protection from urban manifests. Like an animal, he blends with his milieu, bringing pulse to a humdrum world. In search of his hiding place, he creates painted installations for his static effigy. In doing so, he seeks the most profound realism, becoming a pragmatic episode of monotony. Ironically, within in the empty vacuum of repetition, his artificiality renders personification. Thanks to La Gamba, the face of a milk carton is forever changed. Rather than instigating nourishment, opening the fridge will now become the door to a mirror.

In labels, lids and containers, La Gamba appears, his white coat tailored to suit. Yet within his pose lies a sense of mendacity, innate to the many masks stripping him of self. Insatiable, his contagion adheres to no limits, liberating the artist into an omnipresent being. As part of all seen or overlooked, he brings a new face to the everyday, with his stories wryly told. As a whole, he offers a critical or cynical view, raising curiosity within tedium. Some may call him quirky, others just plain odd, but in his idiosyncrasy, he creates a wave of colour, superseding daily rituals.

Aside from effervescence, his work leaves a dismal residue. In his masquerade, La Gamba withdraws from the metropolis, guarded from conformity by his protective skin. This hedonistic artist shows no qualms, yet with his pet-like manner, becomes an emblem of domesticity."

Louise Thompson

Supermarkets

"I first became interested in camouflage as linked to the pleasure of decoy. In nature the life and death importance of proper camouflage as used by animals and insects via mimitism or procrypsis is coupled in art to the revelry of lure. When working on camouflage in my man-made staged settings the only link left between the person who is posing (as in pretending) and the viewer or onlooker (or predator) is the eye. My personal pleasure in painting, photography or in installations remains the same be it with camouflage or hyperrealism: I thrive on "trompe l'oeil" which is a better description of the notion of cheating or deceiving in my work."

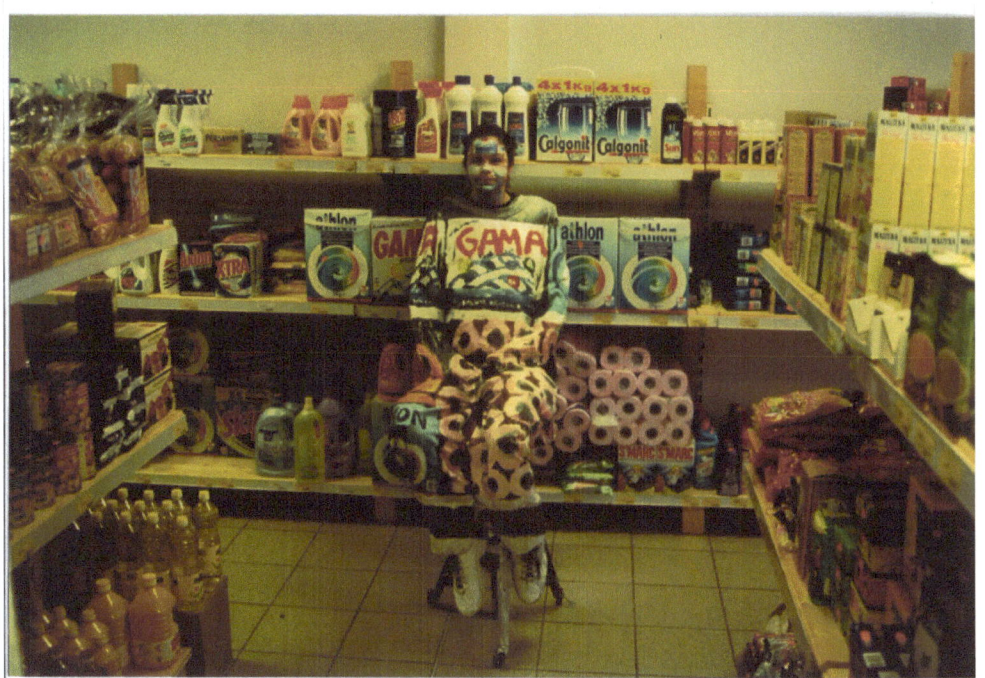

Athlon-Gamma, 2002 Pro-cryptic painting (acrylic on board and protective suit) color photograph, 50 x 75 cm

My analysis of camouflage is not an interpretation of reality. It is not a pictorial symbolization of reality. It is reality. My practice is without concession to its execution or to the methods of its realization. Its execution requires a constant repositioning related to the chromatic transformations of the photosensitive environment. Its practice requires a speed in the execution which varies unceasingly according to the modulations of the various luminous parameters dependent on the atmospheric variations; the produced color being, once created, permanent, and the

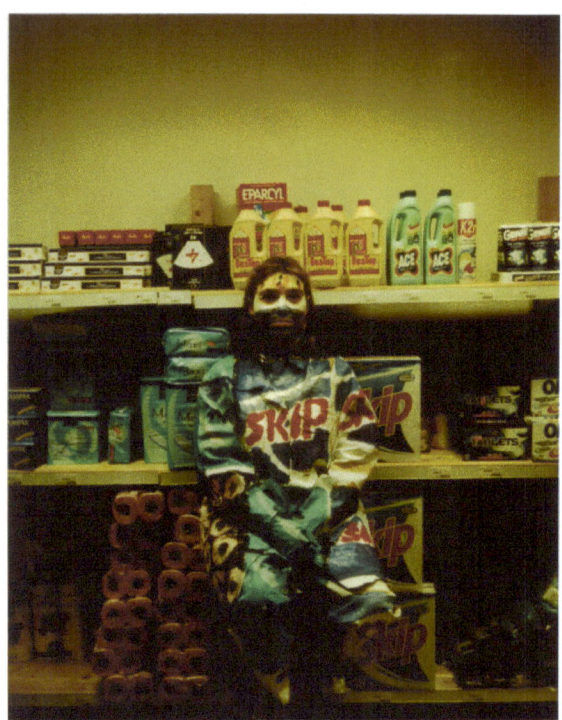

ambient color being the object of permanent modifications. It is necessary to stress that my practice does not consist of an interpretation of colors which are given to be seen in the perception of the chromatic setting, it is not a question of reproduction or homogenization. It is a question of contemplating these colors as they are, as they are without yielding for as much to what is already known of their morphology (it is a tree, a car...) without referring to their potentiality of being a chromatic object influenced by a bond with language. It is a question of reproducing the colors such as they are and not such as we see them. There is also, correlative of my practice, the spectrum of realism (or of hyper-realism) and consequently the temptation to place this execution of camouflage under the angle of a new realism. However, insofar as the practice of the camouflage goes beyond these school codes, it is neither a realism nor a hyper-realism.

Skip, 2002 Pro-cryptic painting (acrylic on board and protective suit) color photograph, 75 x 50 cm

The pictures of urban camouflage intend to show that individuals are characterized by a certain kind of Procrypsis especially in a consumer society such as ours. Volunteers participated in making these installations possible. The latter's aim was to play on the chromatic surge of a supermarkets' visual environment and to artificially merge the individual into this scenery. Volunteers who are people who "belong" to the chosen environment, wear a protective suit, which is then painted as is their face.

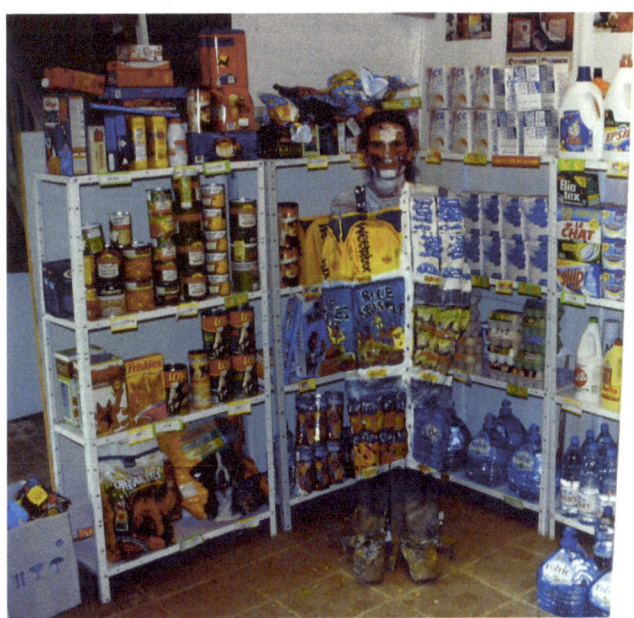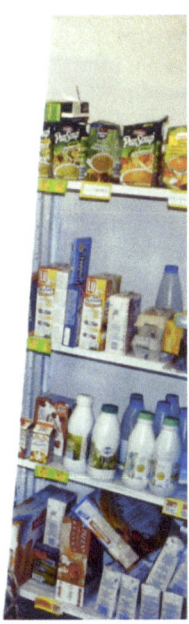

Corner shop, 2002 Pro-cryptic painting (acrylic on board and protective suit) color photograph, 50 x 75 cm

In my photographs the subject is fixed in a cataleptic position of mimitism like the Omega insect on its branch. There is a rupture of any rhythm, the subject finds itself in this fixed position which closely resembles catalepsy. In my installations the bodies of the subjects are fixed, revealing a reinforced hypertonic position which is, amongst other things, caused by the rigid nature of the combination.

For me, this cataleptic 'mise en scene' does not only try to reproduce the mimetic and homeostatic position of the camouflaged animal, but also a kind of ideal position which could simulate the individual in a esthetisation of his social and chromatic motricity reconstituted artificially within his vital space. Of course, this cataleptic constitution is in this case based on a pictorial artifice but this one does not escape the methods of application from the homotypic or homomorphic process which we know from zoology. It is worth to view this 'mise en scene' under the angle of a "visual posture" (of an attire) likely to propose a semiotic of the chromatism of social space.

The cataleptic mimitism creates and follows the discussion on the different visual strategies put in scene by the subjects to answer to the requirements of chromatic integration within a determined space. The camouflage scenes in the urban environment try to unveil these various methodological approaches which, while trying to make the visual segregation null and void, are creating another. Seen from an almost ethnological approach you could say that my pro-cryptic photography drafts the development of a grammar of the urban visuality likely to codify the adaptive chromatic practices of the subject in society through the art of camouflage.

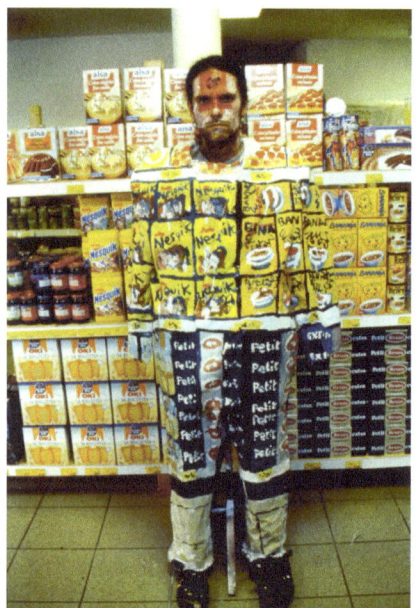 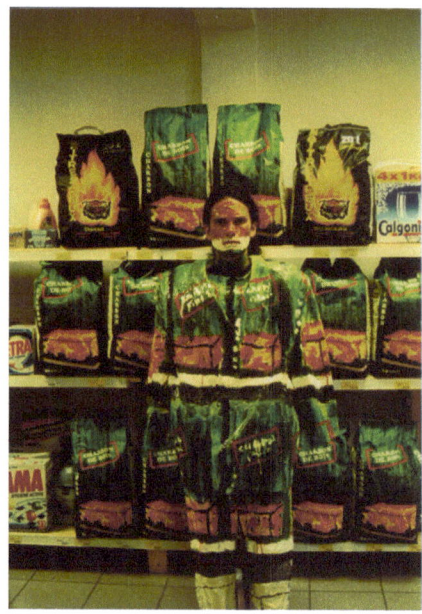

Petits Brun Extra and Charcoal, 2002 Pro-cryptic painting (acrylic on board and protective suit) color photograph, 75 x 50 cm

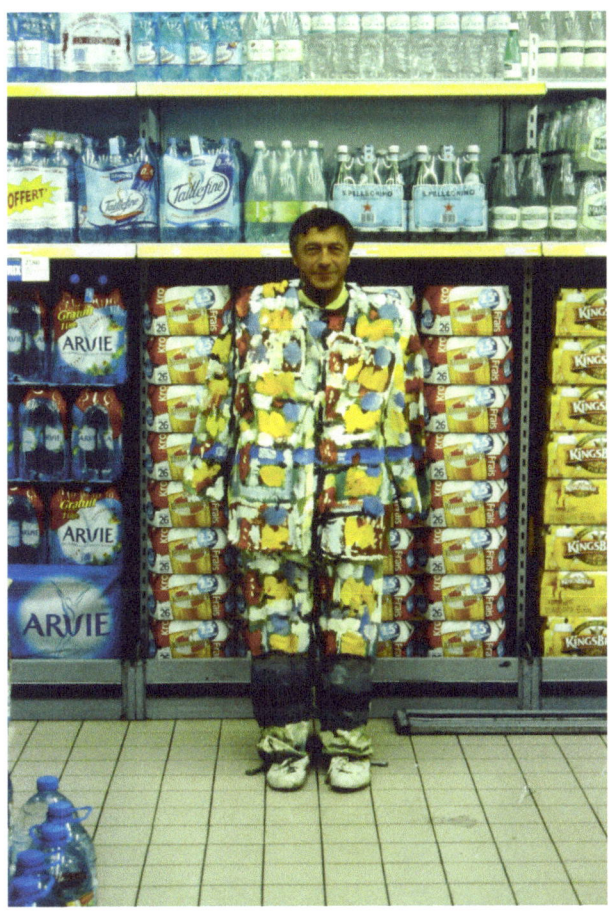

Beer packs, 2002 Pro-cryptic painting (acrylic on board and protective suit) color photograph, 75 x 50 cm

Mimitism is not only a behaviour identified in zoology or in ethology, it is also economic, sociological, biomolecular, and its structural properties exceed by far the sphere of activity of zoology.
I think that it would be necessary to consider the existence of a speciation (within the meaning of an evolution) of the interhuman chromatic reflexes. This chromatic and visual speciation of the subject in his report with social space must be considered as the search for a new chromatic balance by the subject, and through the recomposition by same as the search for a new rebalanced "natural" space.

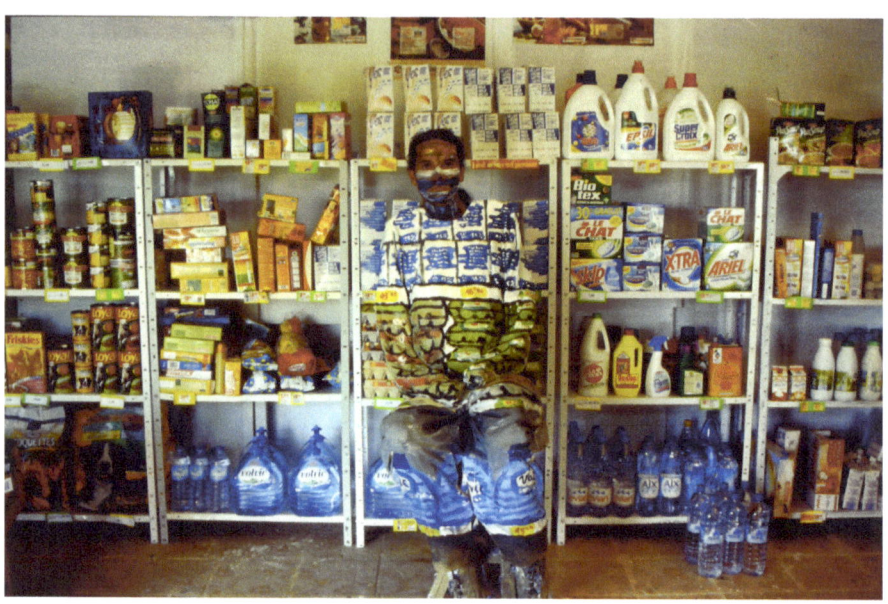

Untitled, 2002 Pro-cryptic painting (acrylic on board and protective suit) color photograph, 50 x 75 cm

But in order to understand the report of man to this desire of speciation, it is necessary to return to the origin of the formation of the ego (and here to take into consideration a number of the stakes raised by my work on self-portraiture (One hundred Self-portraits - 100 Autoportraits, 2000) , to this "Urbild" which is organized around an organic despair correlative to an impossibility for the human being to admit to the possibility of the existence of an environment which is preformed to him. This untenable idea of a natural environment which pre-exists to him (an idea which was already present in pre-Sokrates times), which pre-exists to this absolute narcissistic desire, makes him elude, deny a visual space which is ordered according to two things: the energy devoted to the negation of this medium, and the impossibility of correctly managing what this feeling inherits from the language.

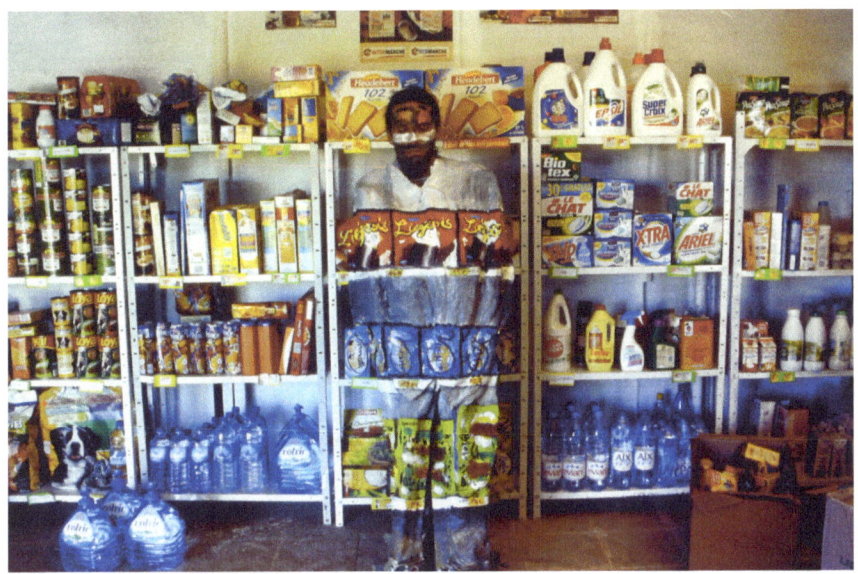

Untitled, 2002 Pro-cryptic painting (acrylic on board and protective suit) color photograph, 50 x 75 cm

I think that it would be necessary to consider the existence of a speciation (within the meaning of an evolution) of the interhuman chromatic reflexes. This chromatic and visual speciation of the subject in his report with social space must be considered as the search for a new chromatic balance by the subject, and through the recomposition by same as the search for a new rebalanced "natural" space.
But in order to understand the report of man to this desire of speciation, it is necessary to return to the origin of the formation of the ego (and here to take into

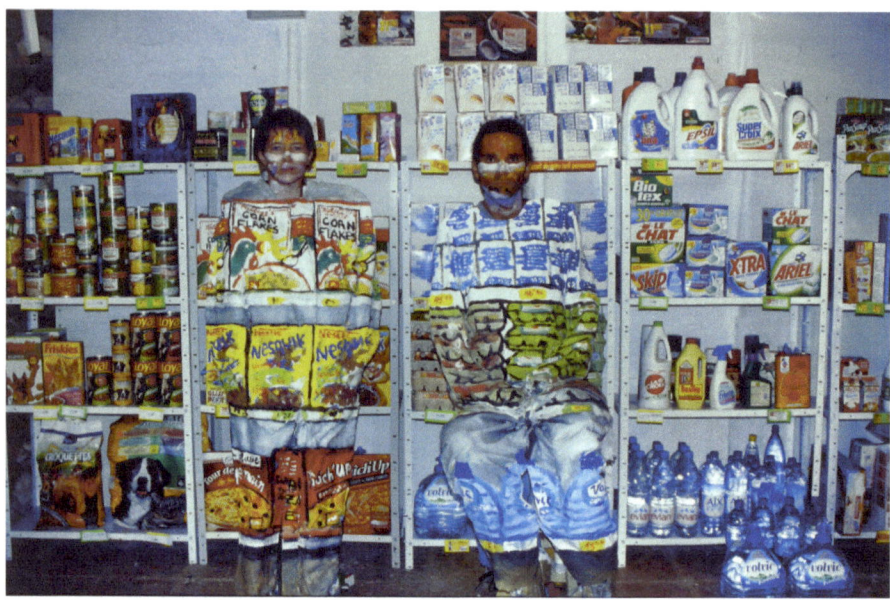

consideration a number of the stakes raised by my work on self-portraiture (One hundred Self-portraits - 100 Autoportraits, 2000) , to this "Urbild" which is organized around an organic despair correlative to an impossibility for the human being to admit to the possibility of the existence of an environment which is preformed to him. This untenable idea of a natural environment which pre-exists to him (an idea which was already present in pre-Sokrates times), which pre-exists to this absolute narcissistic desire, makes him elude, deny a visual space which is ordered according to two things: the energy devoted to the negation of this medium, and the impossibility of correctly managing what this feeling inherits from the language.

Untitled, 2002 Pro-cryptic painting (acrylic on board and protective suit) color photograph, 50 x 75 cm

My work " Pet food " does not mean "Dog food" it is " Pet food " and calls on this evocative power of the significant... and what specifies man, in the sense of what makes his species is when he more or less successfully manages to impress his image on reality. It is this narcissistic and fundamentally alienating basis which is also questioned by my photography, through the means of camouflage slightly accentuating the narcissistic position of the subject in a medium in which it "will never completely be integrated" and in which visual and homochromatic integration is the basis of its narcissistic desire.

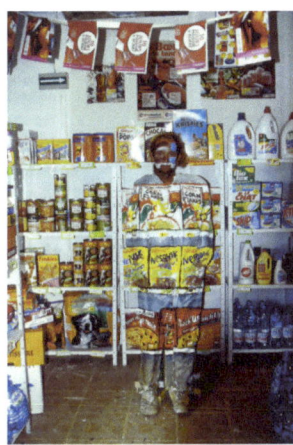 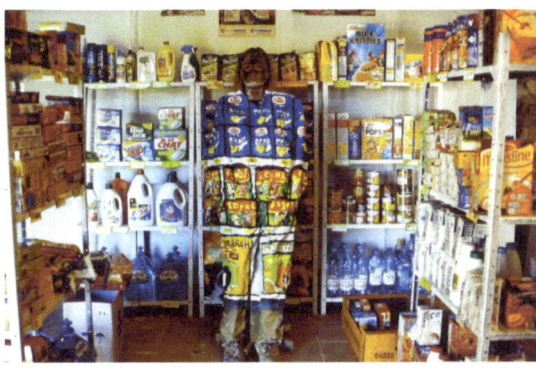

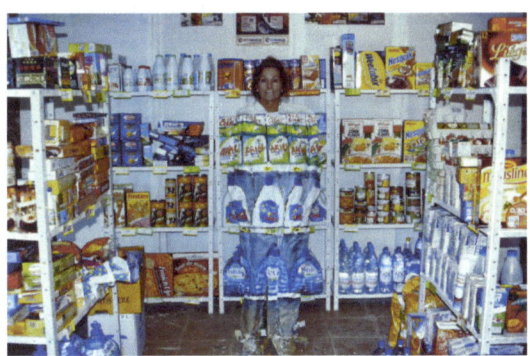 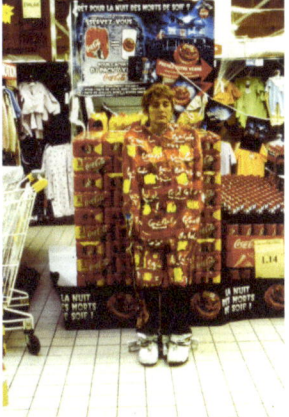

Untitled and Halloween, 2002 Pro-cryptic painting (acrylic on board and protective suit) color photograph, 75 x 50 cm

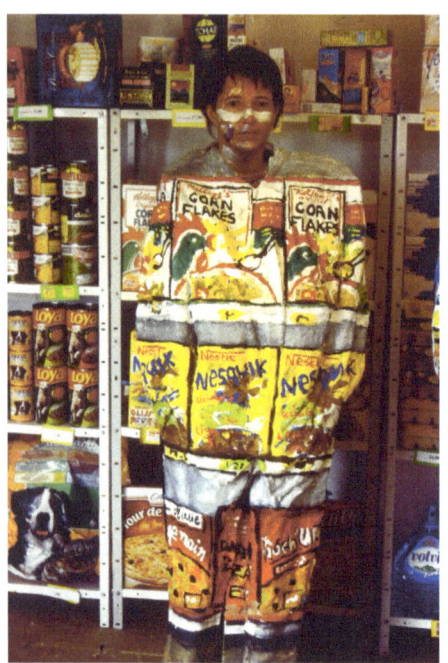
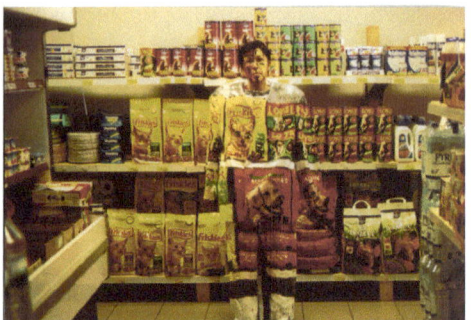
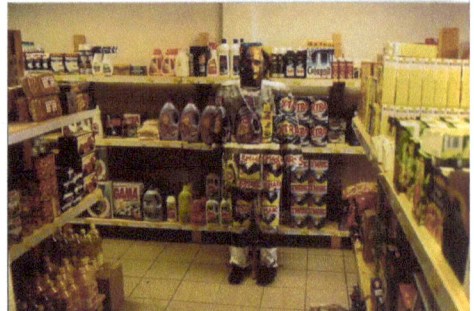

Pet Food, 2002 Pro-cryptic painting (acrylic on board and protective suit) color photograph, 75 x 50 cm

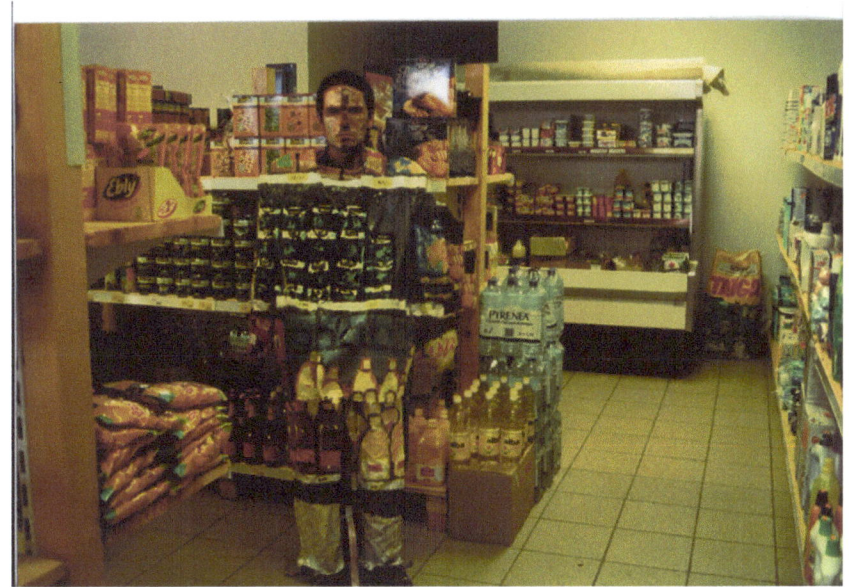

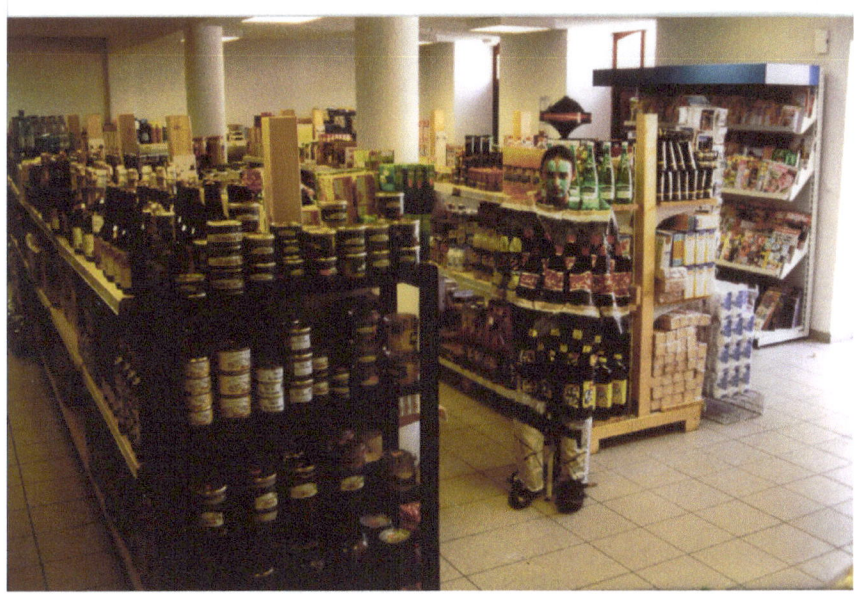

Mixed vegetables and Ice tea, 2002 Pro-cryptic painting (acrylic on board and protective suit) color photograph, 50 x 75 cm

Open fridge series

The "reality of the appearance" visualizes also the end of the so-called centralized subject, symbolized by the primacy of mechanical reproduction, as in this case assumed by the presence of the Open Fridge (Appliances).

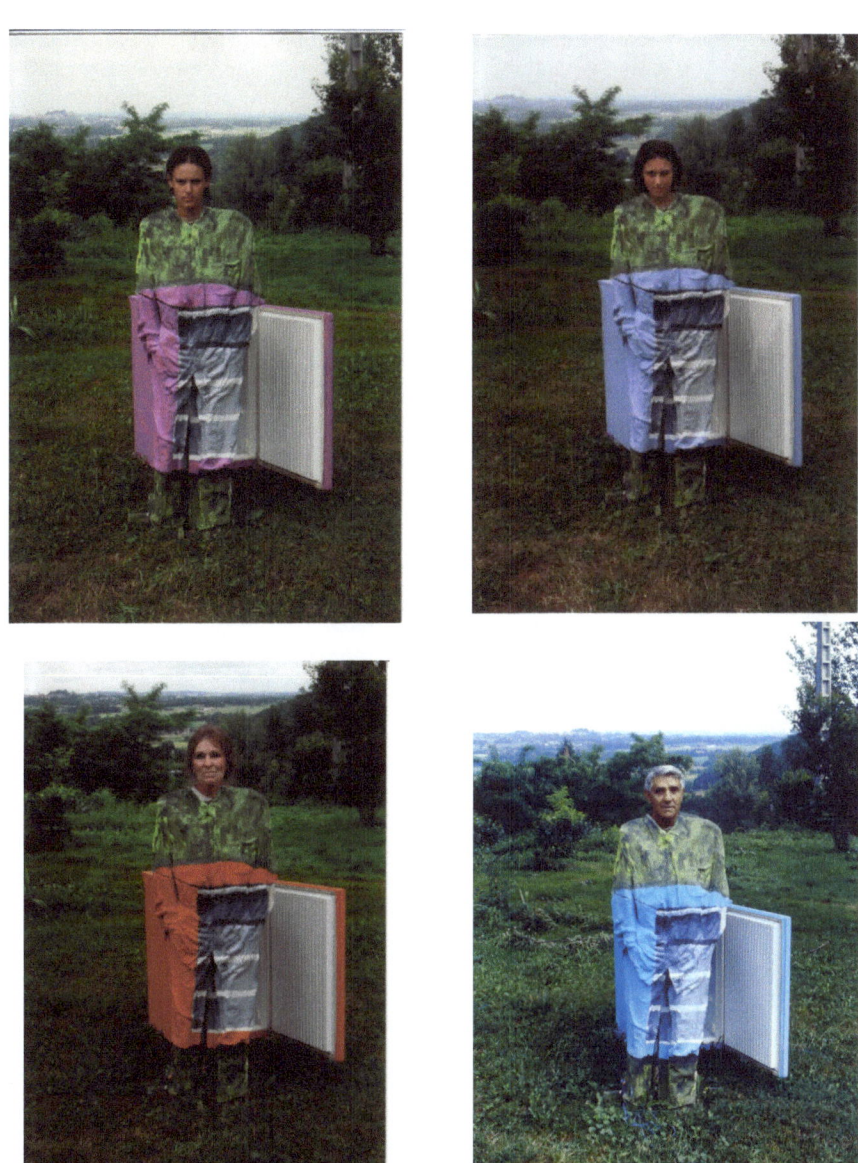

Open fridge, 2002 Pro-cryptic painting (acrylic on board and protective suit) color
photograph, 75 x 50 cm

" My "Open Fridge" series attempts to visualize the question of the body in its relationship to the machine - a relationship between the body and the particular sort of object which a machine is, and whose symbolism has often been put forward as a mirror of man himself. From the very first clocks up to mechanical, electrical, electronic or digital 'machines' one uses daily (washing machine, dish-washer) there has been, on some level, a longing to draw a parallel between man and the machine if only because of the way body and machine work (pumping, ticking, beating emptying, filling, breaking down, dying…). My work suggests a common mold for man and machine, a pictorial translation of this unnatural relationship. These installations remove the machine from its environment and link it to the 'other' body.

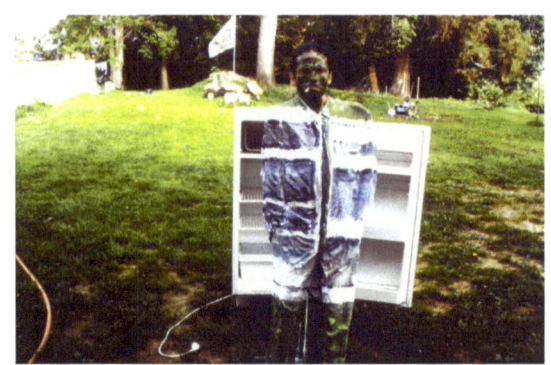

In his 1955 article entitled "Freud, Hegel and the Machine", Jacques Lacan revealed and analysed how comparing a body to a machine was a mistake. Breaking down the body to analyze or fix it as if it were a machine (something that according to Lacan went back to Huyghens' clocks) enabled some people to underhandedly compare the kinetic energy of the body to the mechanisms of the machine. The Open Fridge series focuses on the mirage of man's body being or striving to be well-oiled and homeostatic. With the Open-Fridge, (Open cooker, Open washing-machine) project my aim was to create a man/machine group and to show that only this obscene hybrid is well-regulated and balanced, has no highs or lows, simply put: has no symptoms…"

"About Open Fridges: Man, The Machine and the kinetic energy Myth", Laurent La Gamba, April 2002.

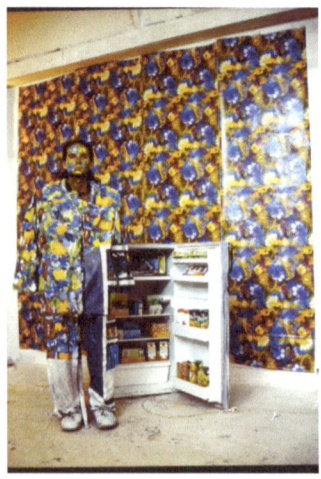

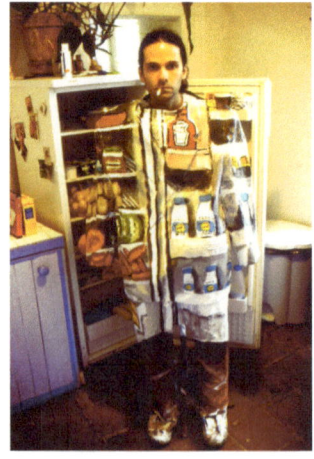

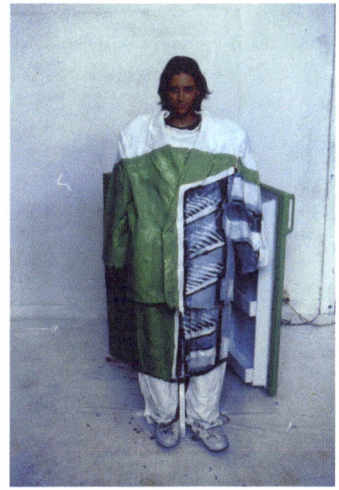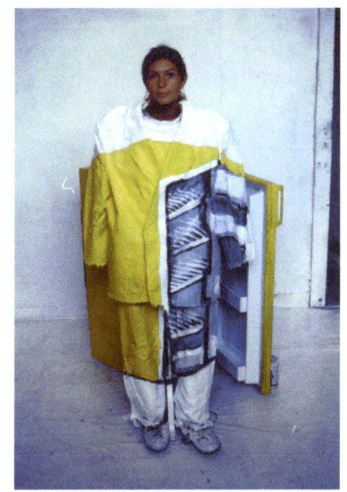
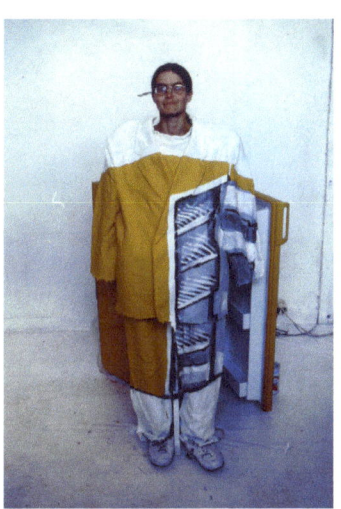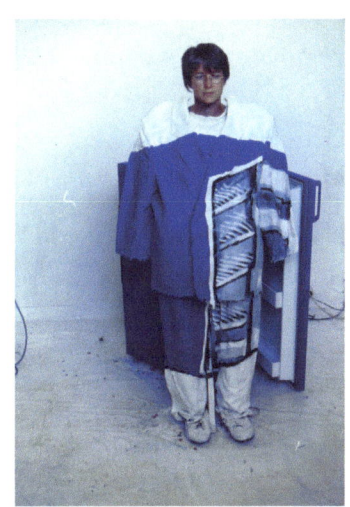

Open fridge, 2002 Pro-cryptic painting (acrylic on board and protective suit) color photograph, 75 x 50 cm

My photography (since it draws its specificity from using a very visually connoted social background) has often been interpreted as conveying a social criticism

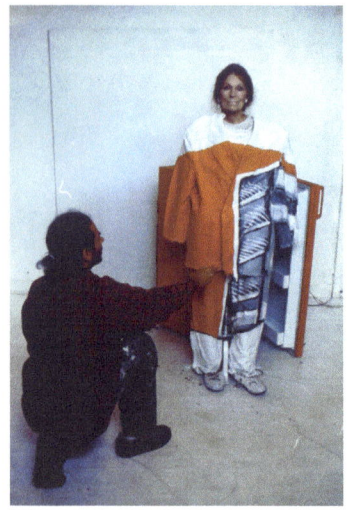 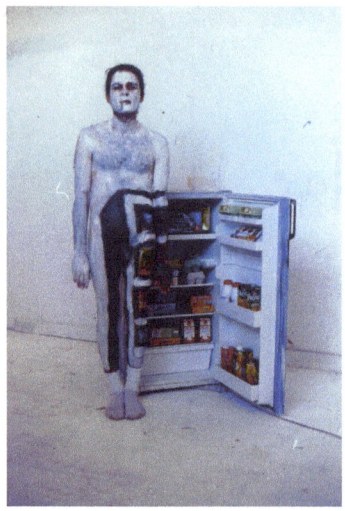

insisting on some alienating aspects of social space (or additionally because it uses objects from the environment of consumption, very connoted in respect to their social function; see Open Fridges and Washing Machines) as if I wished to produce a critical discussion on mass consumption with a tendency to show how this space itself not only contains but also creates an alienating element. Neither of it is true. This social space does not create the alienation, it was present from the beginning. These spaces without transitions constitute a symbolic proposal of nature to overcome this fundamental scopic alienation. This is why, even if my photography

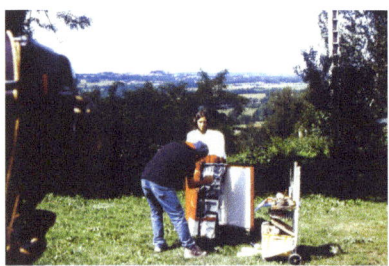 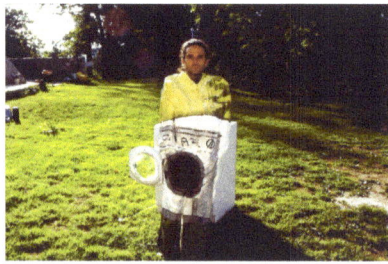

allows a possibility of analysis under the angle of sociology, it offers a prospect for more complete study if it is considered under the phenomenological and behavioural angle.

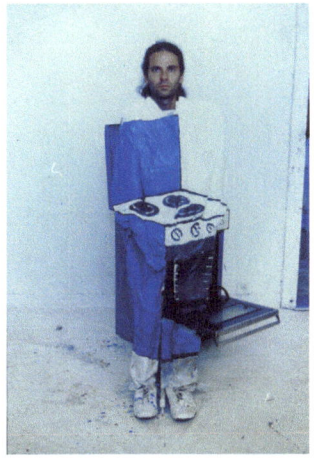 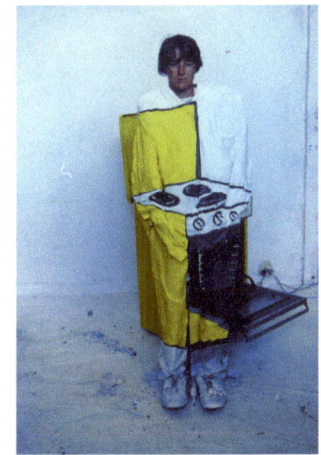

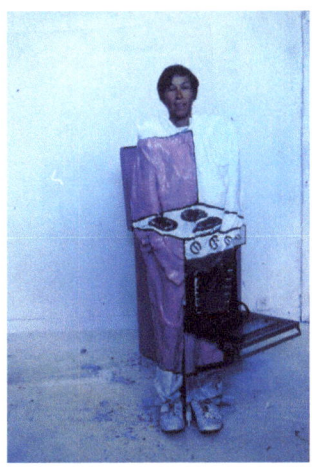 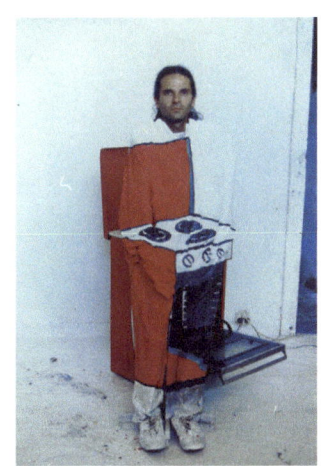

Cookers, 2002 Pro-cryptic painting (acrylic on board and protective suit) color photograph, 75 x 50 cm

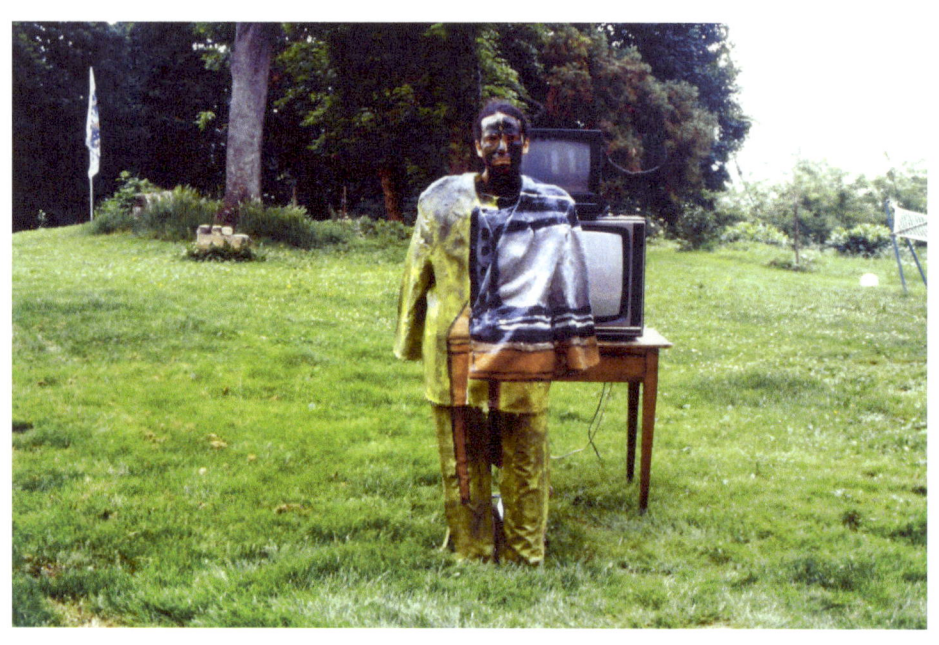

Appliances, 2004 Pro-cryptic painting (acrylic on board and protective suit) color photograph, 50 x 75 cm

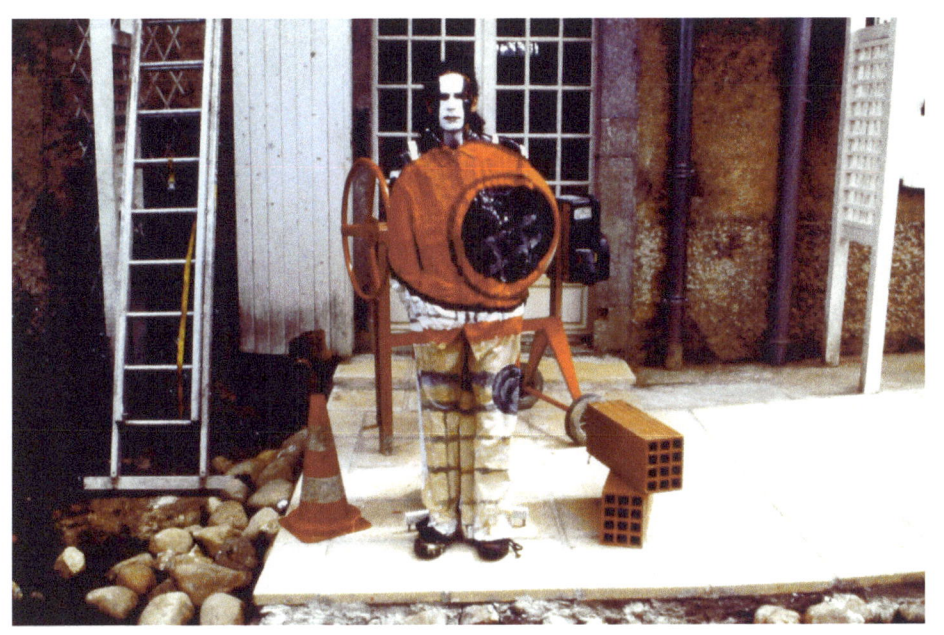

Concrete mixer, 2003 Pro-cryptic painting (acrylic on board and protective suit)
color photograph, 50 x 75 cm

Studio works

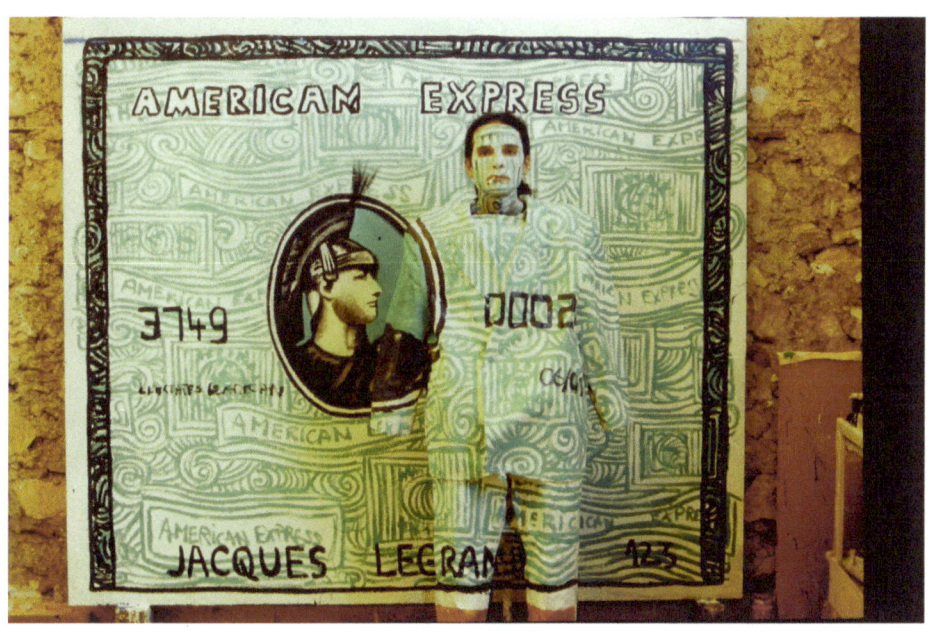

Self-portrait as an American Express card, 2002 Pro-cryptic painting (acrylic on board and protective suit) color photograph, 50 x 75 cm

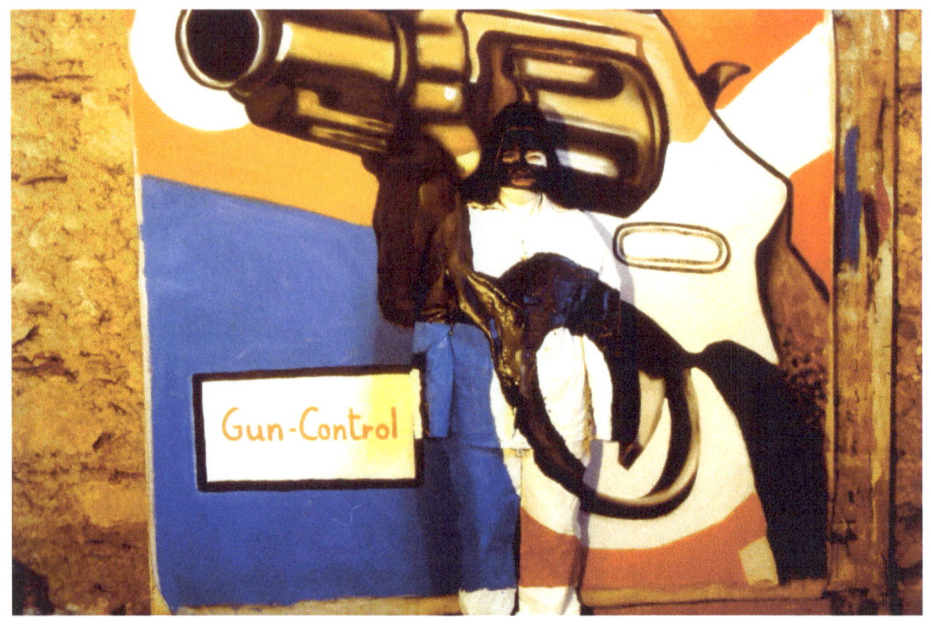

Gun Control, 2002 Pro-cryptic painting (acrylic on board and protective suit) color photograph, 50 x 75 cm

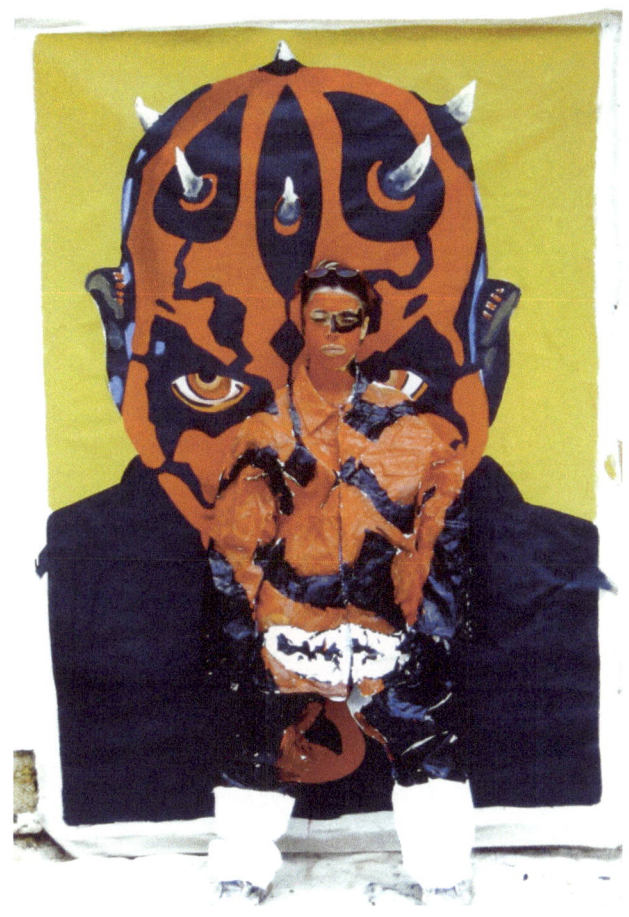

Untitled, 2002 Pro-cryptic painting (acrylic on board and protective suit) color photograph, 75 x 50 cm

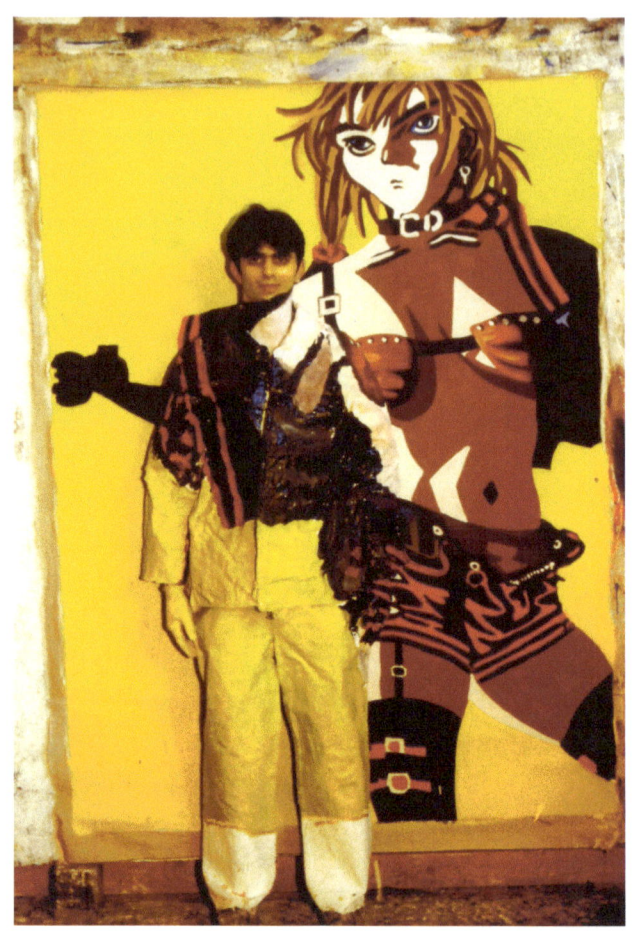

Manga, 2002 Pro-cryptic painting (acrylic on board and protective suit) color photograph, 75 x 50 cm

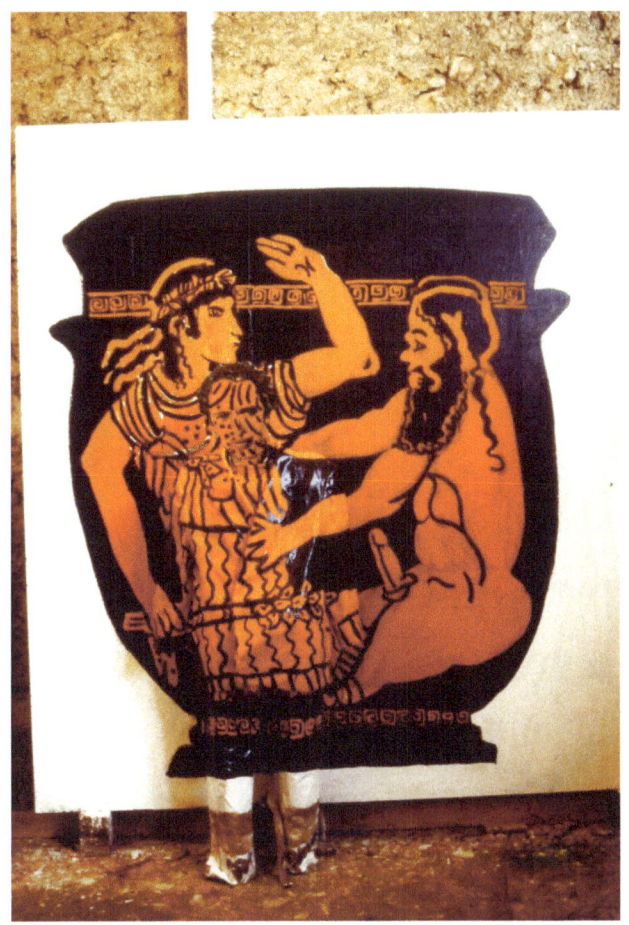

Untitled, 2003, Pro-cryptic painting (acrylic on board and protective suit) color photograph, 75 x 50 cm

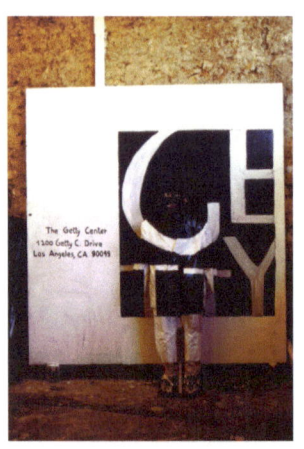
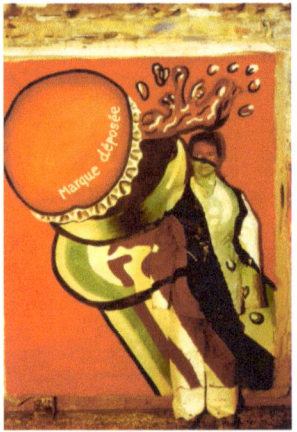
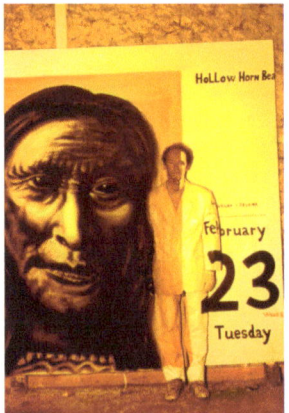
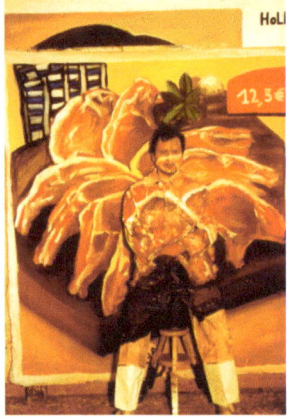

Untitled, 2002 Pro-cryptic painting (acrylic on board and protective suit) color
photograph, 75 x 50 cm

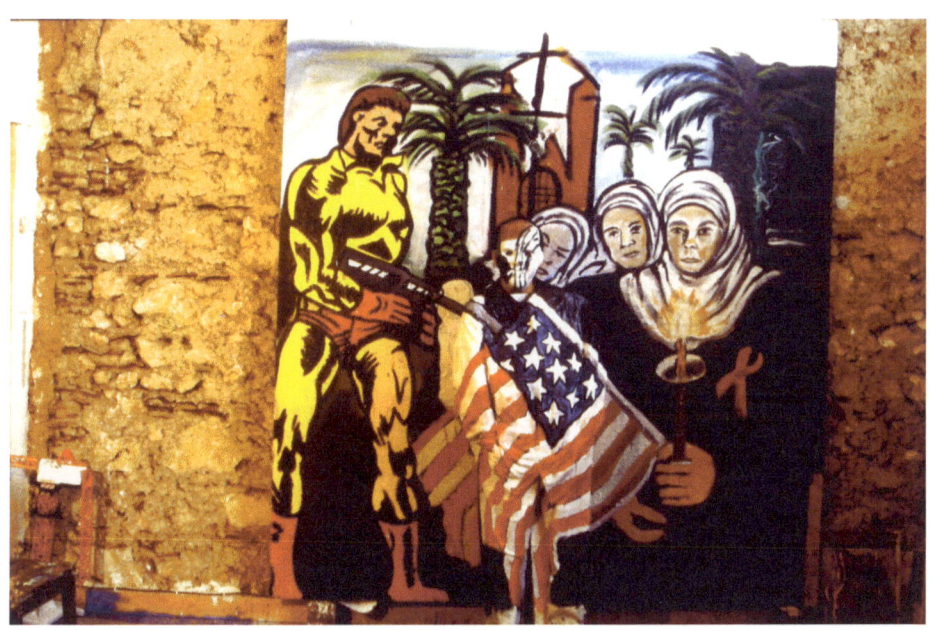

9/11 series, 2002 Pro-cryptic painting (acrylic on board and protective suit) color photograph, 75 x 50 cm

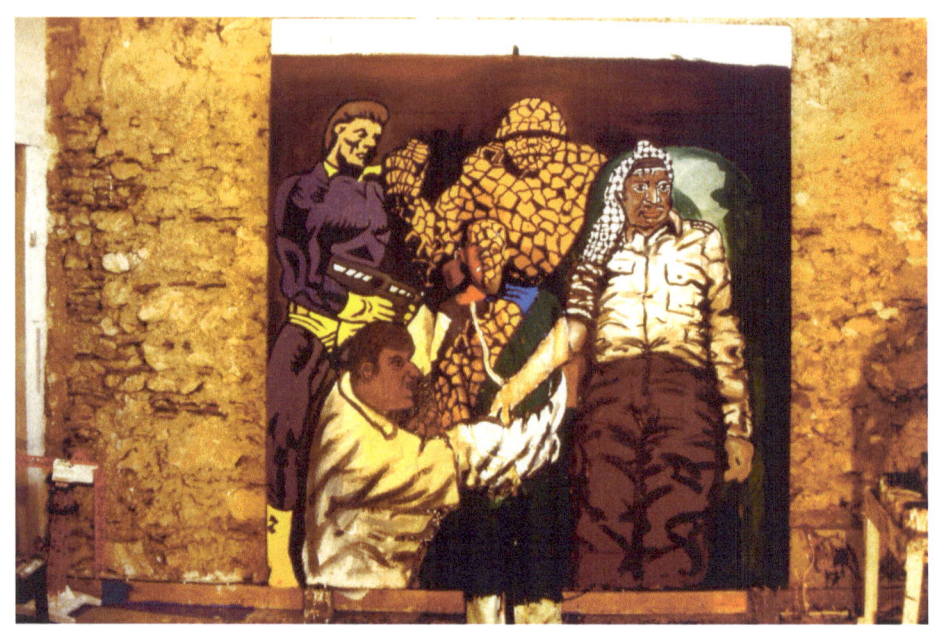

9/11 series, 2002 Pro-cryptic painting (acrylic on board and protective suit) color photograph, 75 x 50 cm

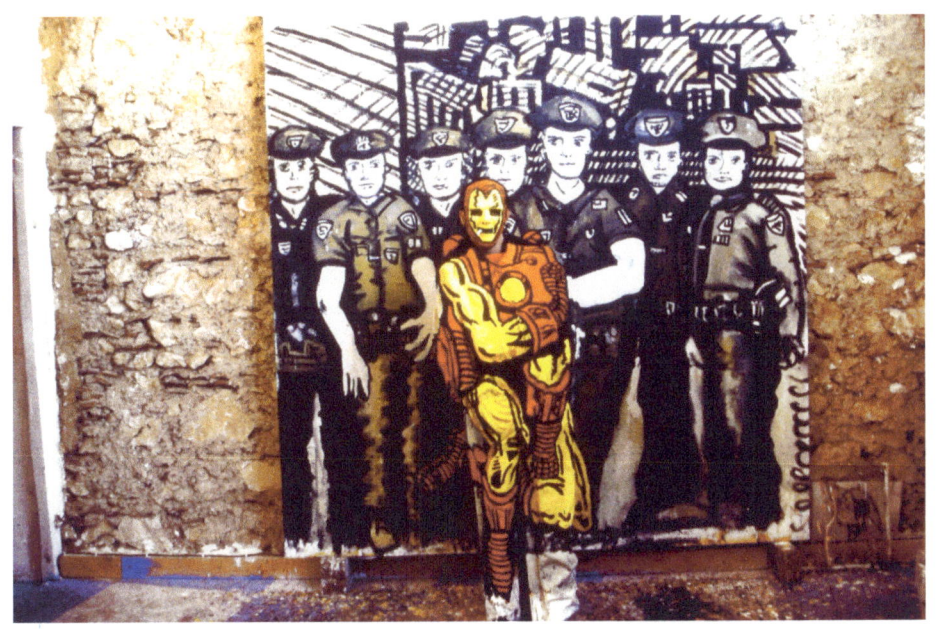

9/11 series, 2002 Pro-cryptic painting (acrylic on board and protective suit) color
photograph, 75 x 50 cm

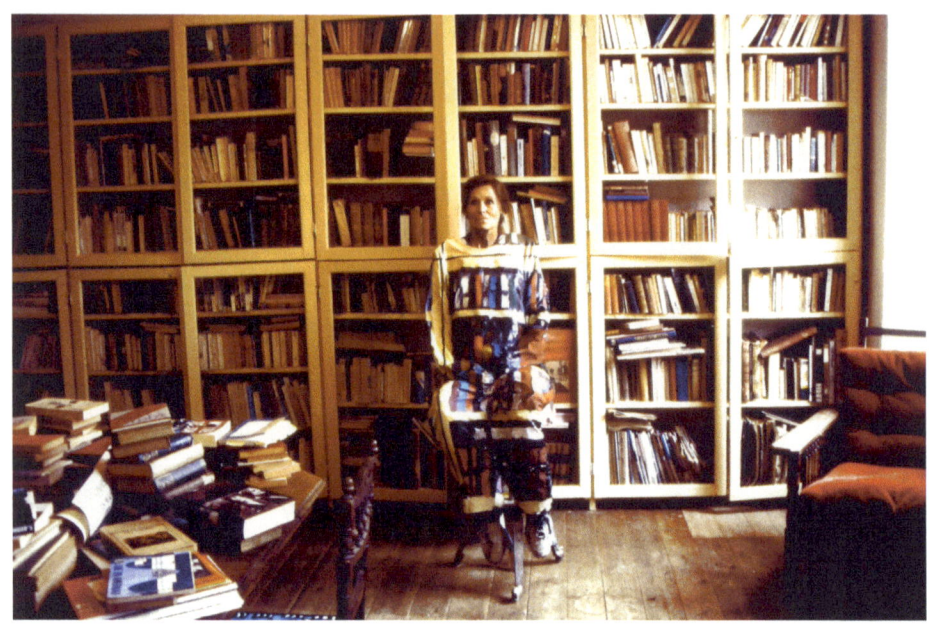

Untitled, 2002 Pro-cryptic painting (acrylic on board and protective suit) color
photograph, 75 x 50 cm

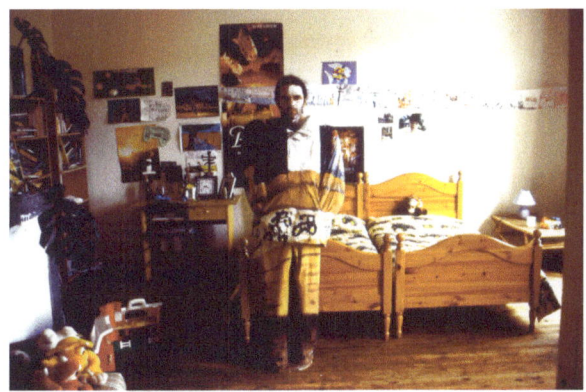

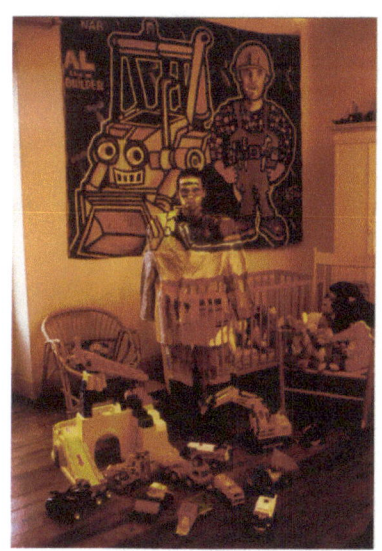

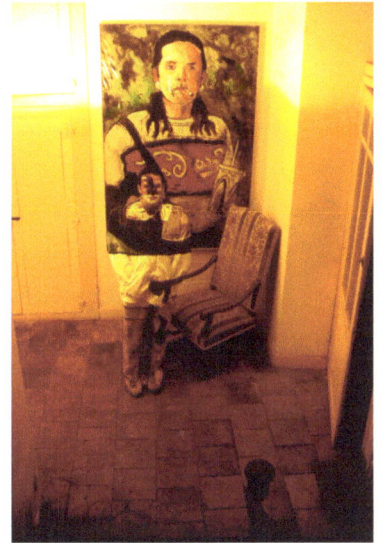

Untitled, 2002 Pro-cryptic painting (acrylic on board and protective suit) color photograph, 75 x 50 cm

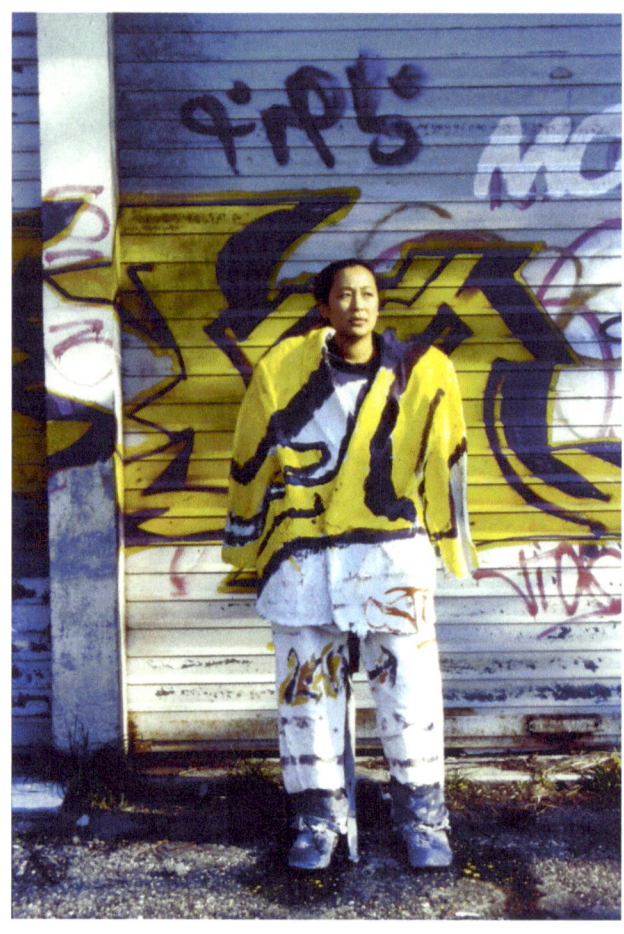

Graffiti, 2002 Pro-cryptic painting (acrylic on board and protective suit) color
photograph, 75 x 50 cm

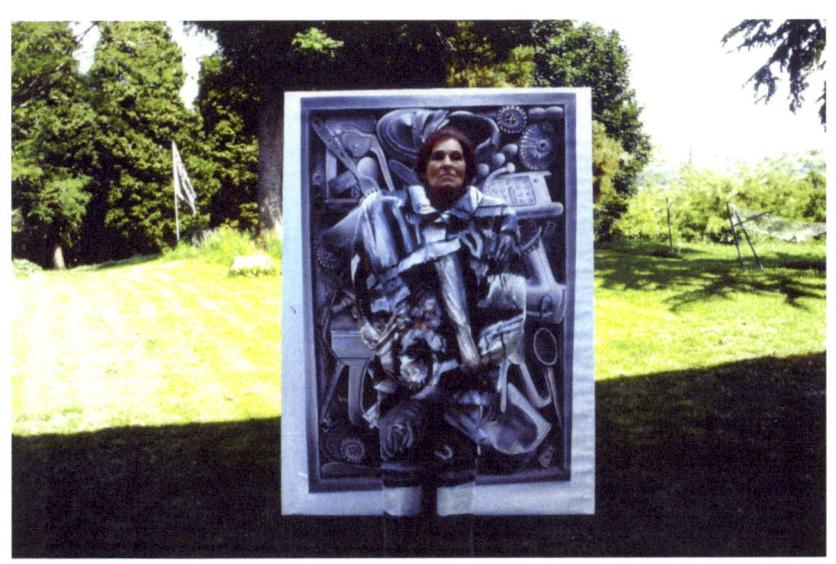

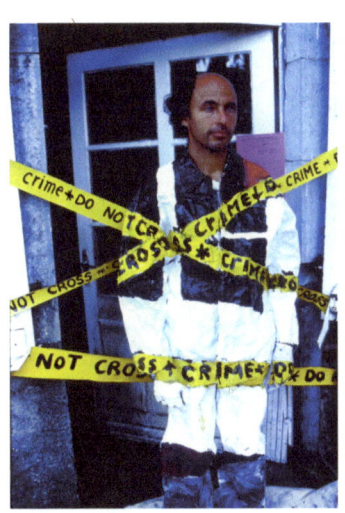

Do not cross, crime scene, 2002 Pro-cryptic painting (acrylic on board and protective suit) color photograph, 75 x 50 cm

Cars

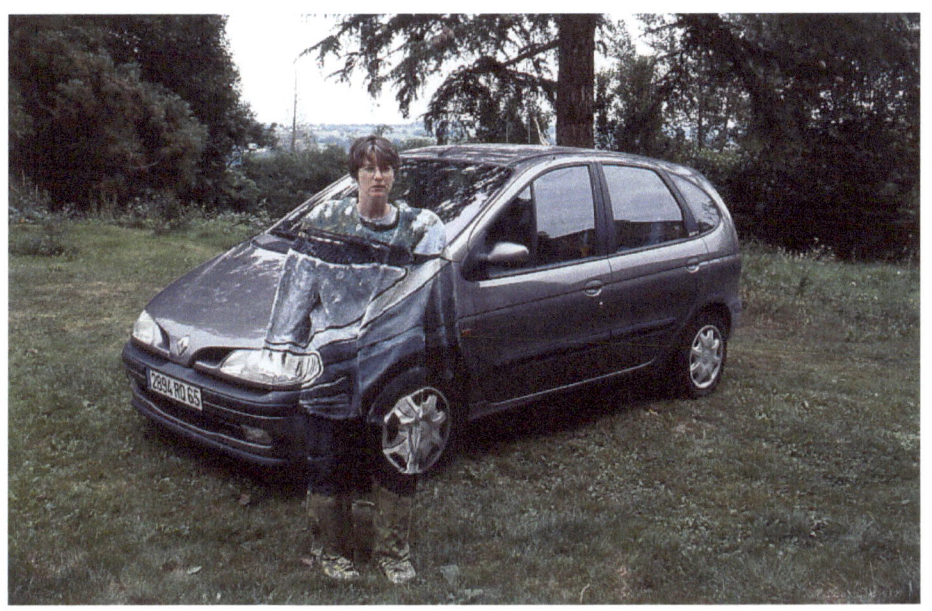

Car series, 2002 Pro-cryptic painting (acrylic on board and protective suit) color photograph, 75 x 50 cm

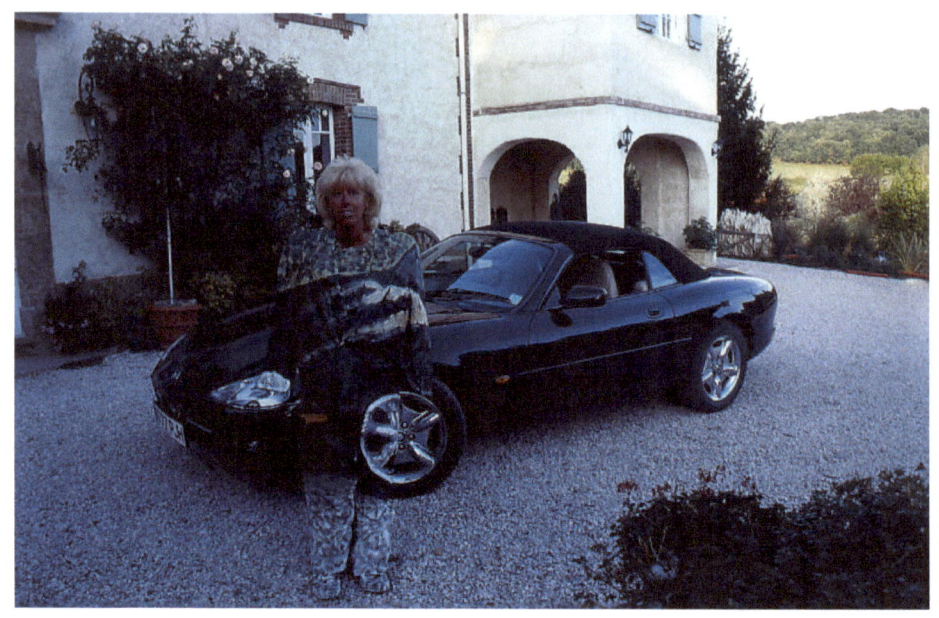

Car series, 2002 Pro-cryptic painting (acrylic on board and protective suit) color photograph, 75 x 50 cm

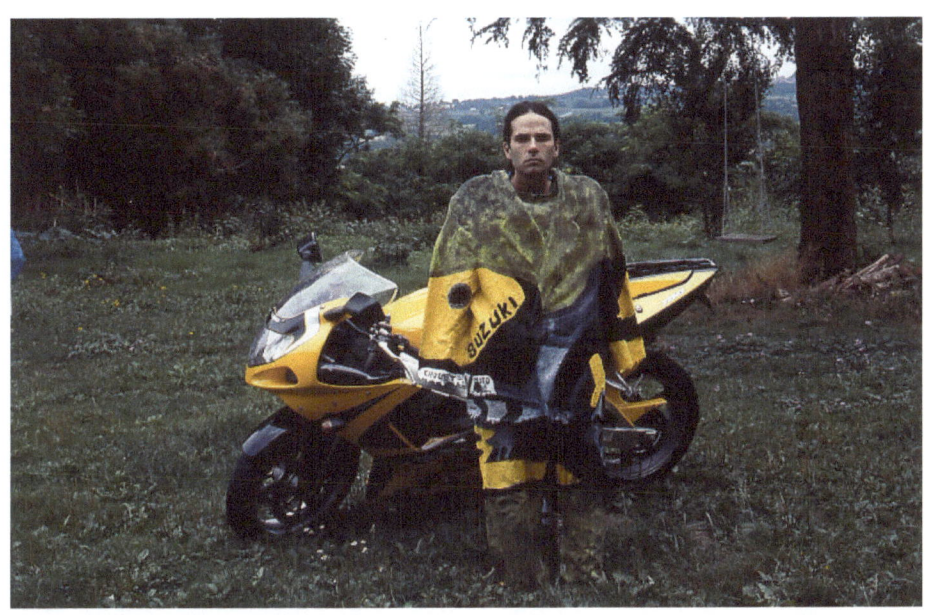

Car series, 2002 Pro-cryptic painting (acrylic on board and protective suit) color photograph, 75 x 50 cm

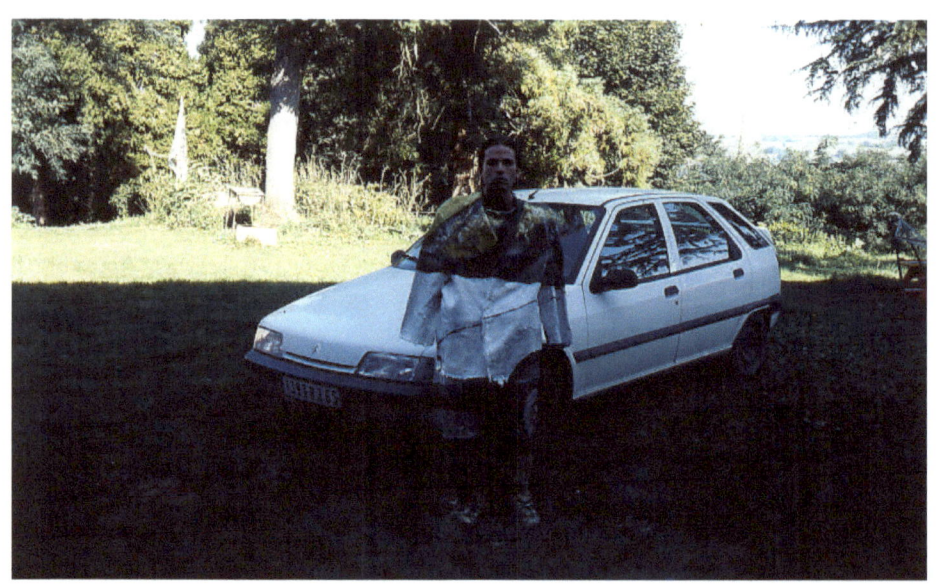

Car series, 2002 Pro-cryptic painting (acrylic on board and protective suit) color photograph, 75 x 50 cm

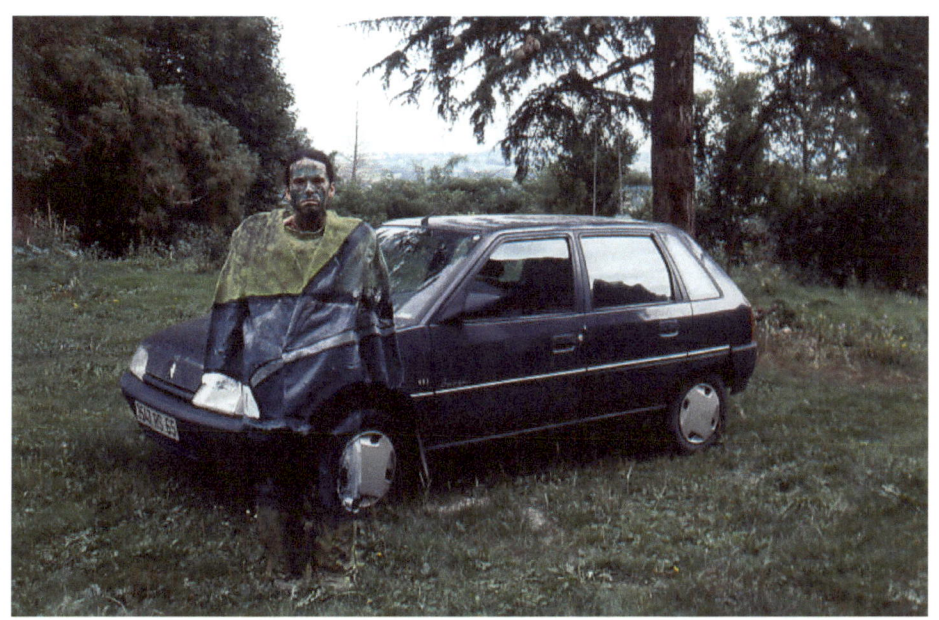

Car series, 2002 Pro-cryptic painting (acrylic on board and protective suit) color photograph, 75 x 50 cm

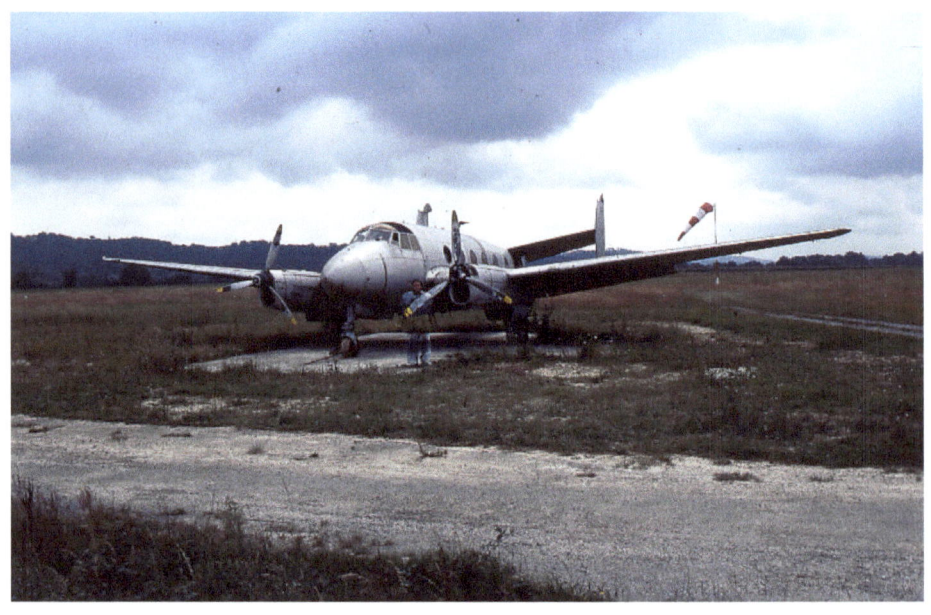

Untitled, 2002 Pro-cryptic painting (acrylic on board and protective suit) color
photograph, 75 x 50 cm

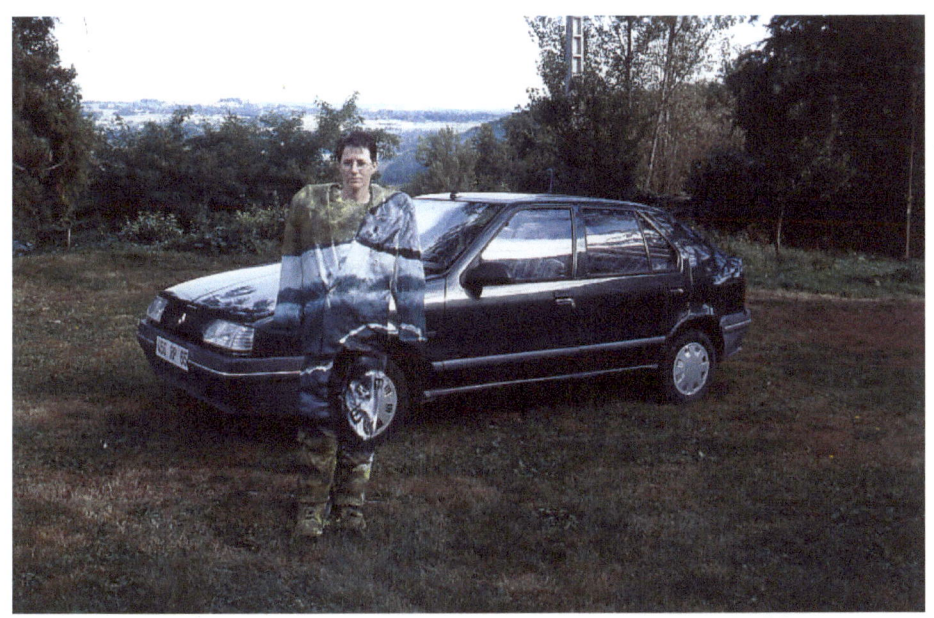

Car series, 2002 Pro-cryptic painting (acrylic on board and protective suit) color photograph, 75 x 50 cm

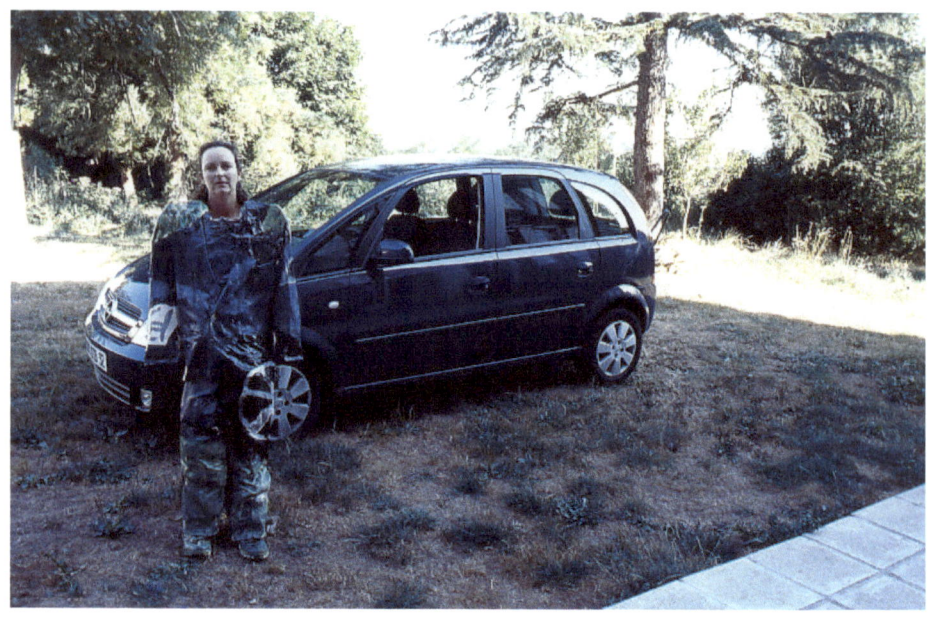

Car series, 2002 Pro-cryptic painting (acrylic on board and protective suit) color photograph, 75 x 50 cm

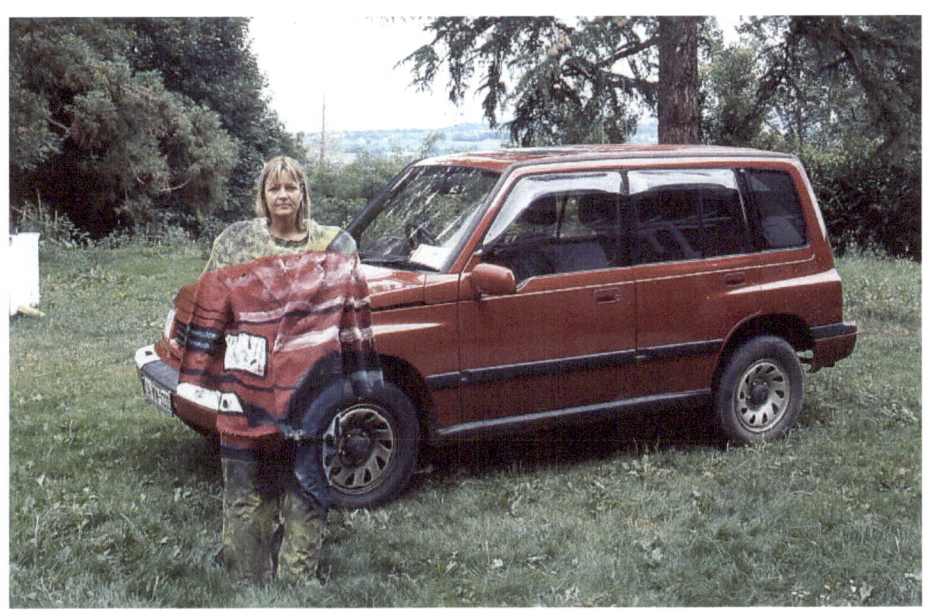

Car series, 2002 Pro-cryptic painting (acrylic on board and protective suit) color photograph, 75 x 50 cm

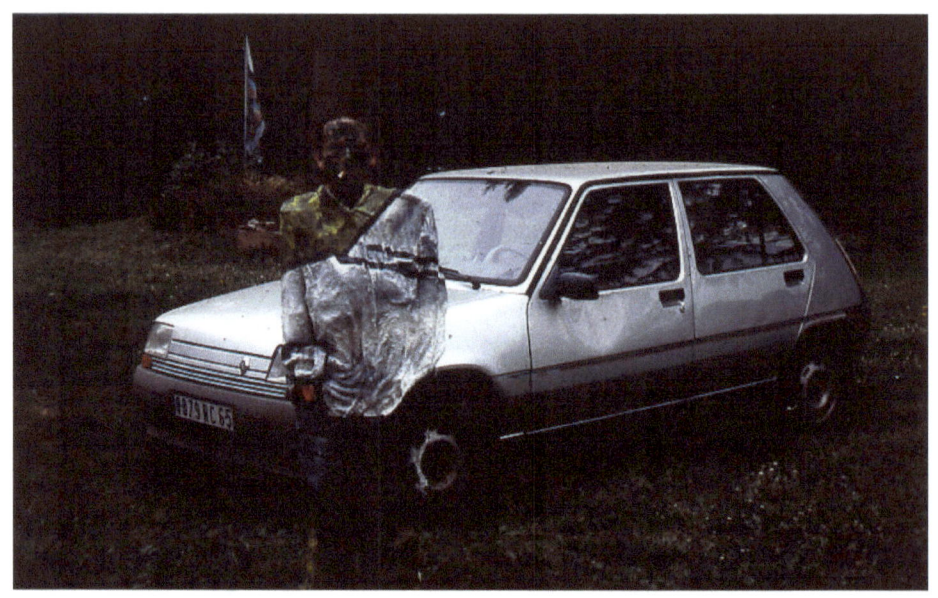

Car series, 2002 Pro-cryptic painting (acrylic on board and protective suit) color photograph, 75 x 50 cm

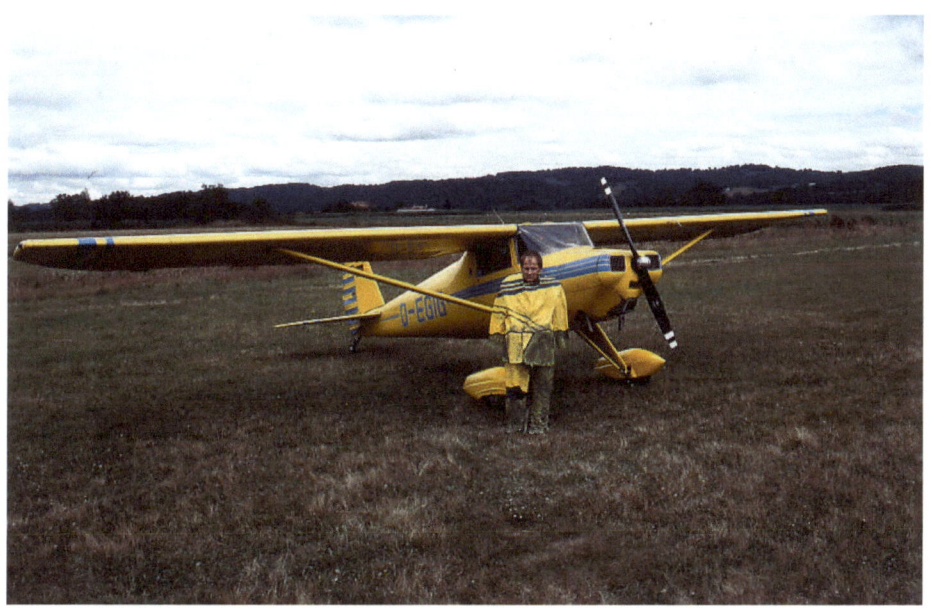

Yellow plane, 2002 Pro-cryptic painting (acrylic on board and protective suit) color photograph, 75 x 50 cm

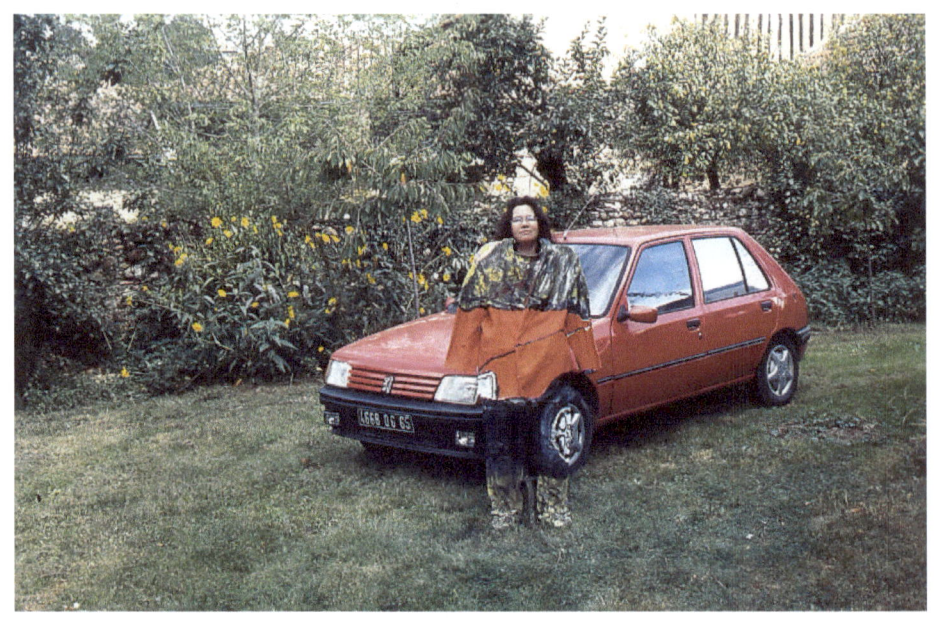

Car series, 2002 Pro-cryptic painting (acrylic on board and protective suit) color photograph, 75 x 50 cm

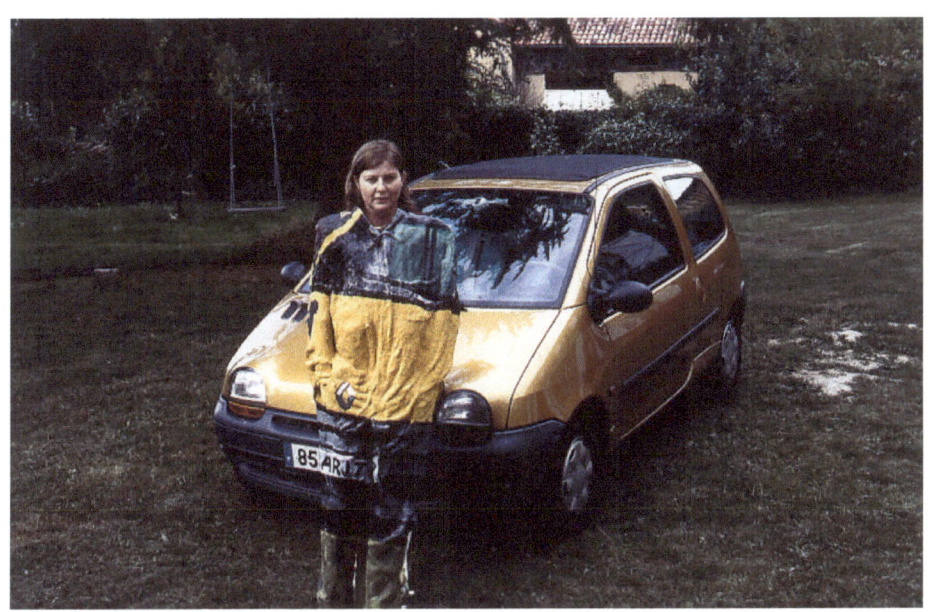

Car series, 2002 Pro-cryptic painting (acrylic on board and protective suit) color photograph, 75 x 50 cm

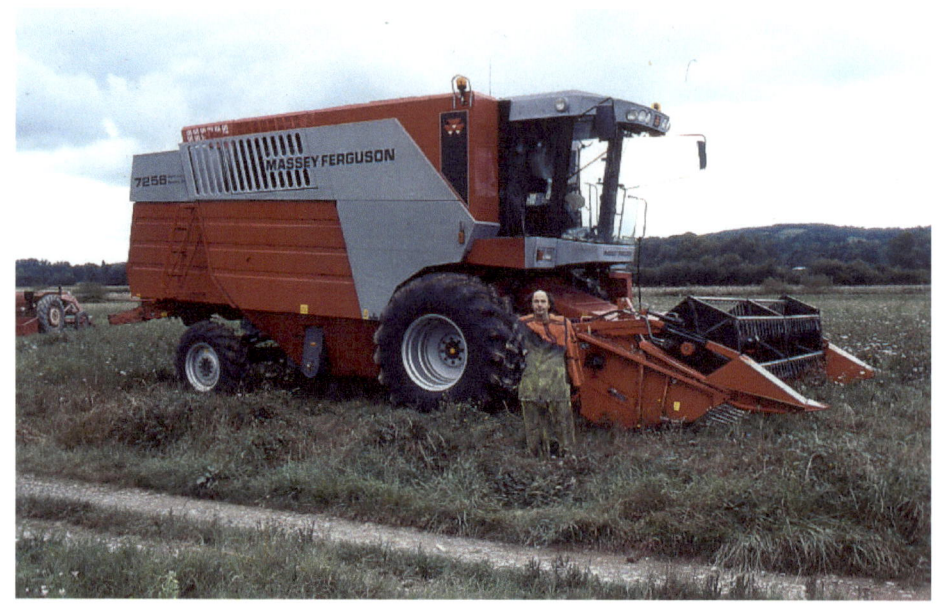

Untitled, 2002 Pro-cryptic painting (acrylic on board and protective suit) color photograph, 75 x 50 cm

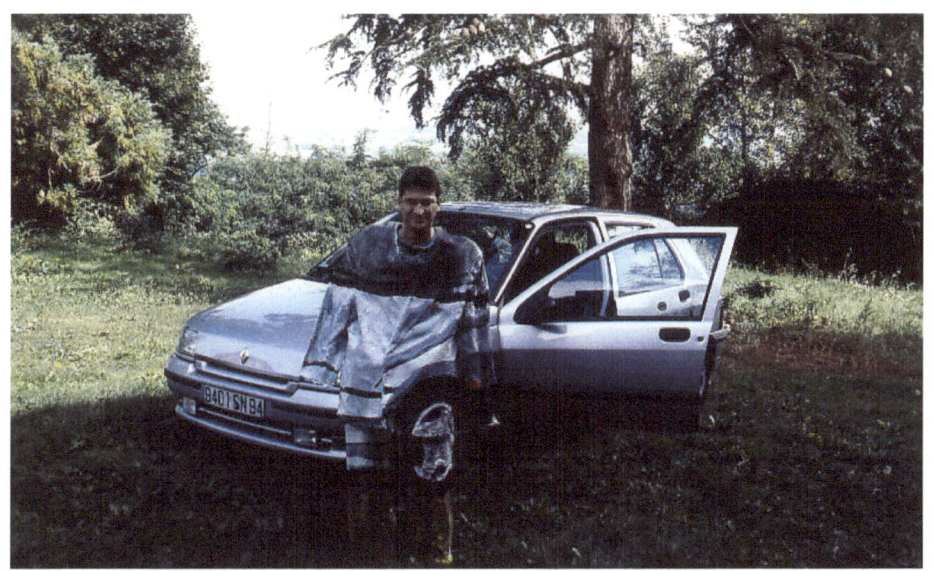

Car series, 2002 Pro-cryptic painting (acrylic on board and protective suit) color photograph, 75 x 50 cm

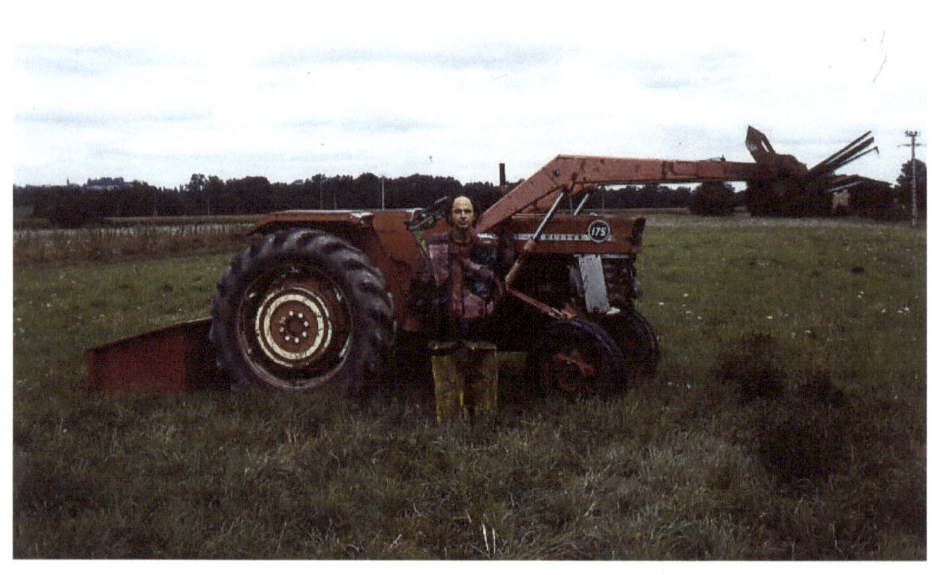

Untitled, 2002 Pro-cryptic painting (acrylic on board and protective suit) color photograph, 75 x 50 cm

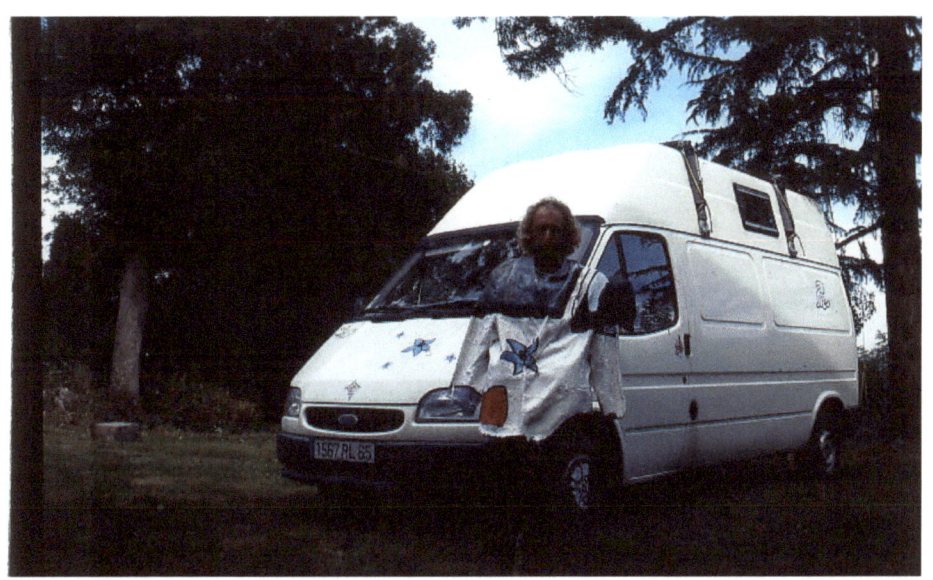

Car series, 2002 Pro-cryptic painting (acrylic on board and protective suit) color photograph, 75 x 50 cm

Swimming-pools

"During the summer of 2003 I started camouflageing a series of people, friends, and friends of friends, who are owners of a swimming-pool in the area I live in.
And then, progressively, the series has started to take a life of its own, and I have found myself with around 30 photographs representing people, all camouflaged with their pool, or, to be specific, camouflaged in front of the refrigerator that I positioned at the pool. This series reintroduces certain elements that were a content/theme in my high-gloss analysis series. Both series are introducing an element into a setting where it doesn't belong and was never meant to be a part of. Each model/

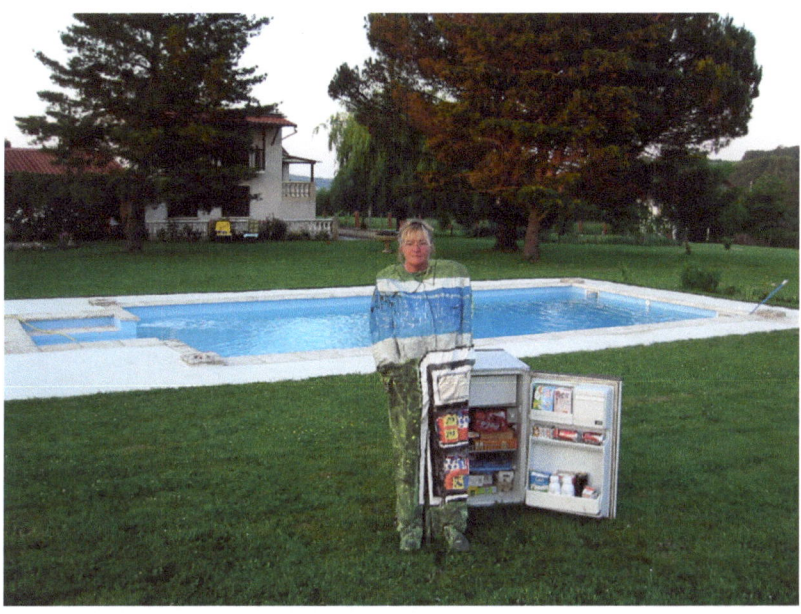

Swimming-pool, 2003 Pro-cryptic painting (acrylic on board and protective suit) color photograph, 75 x 50 cm

photographed person is the owner of the respective pool, in the sense of him being the one to appreciate and enjoy the use of that swimming-pool, but also, in the other sense of the word, the joy of being the owner of a swimming-pool.

As opposed to the high-gloss analysis, where the unexpected and foreign element of the photograph is caused by the image of a household appliance set within a landscape, two completely unconnected elements joined together, we do find

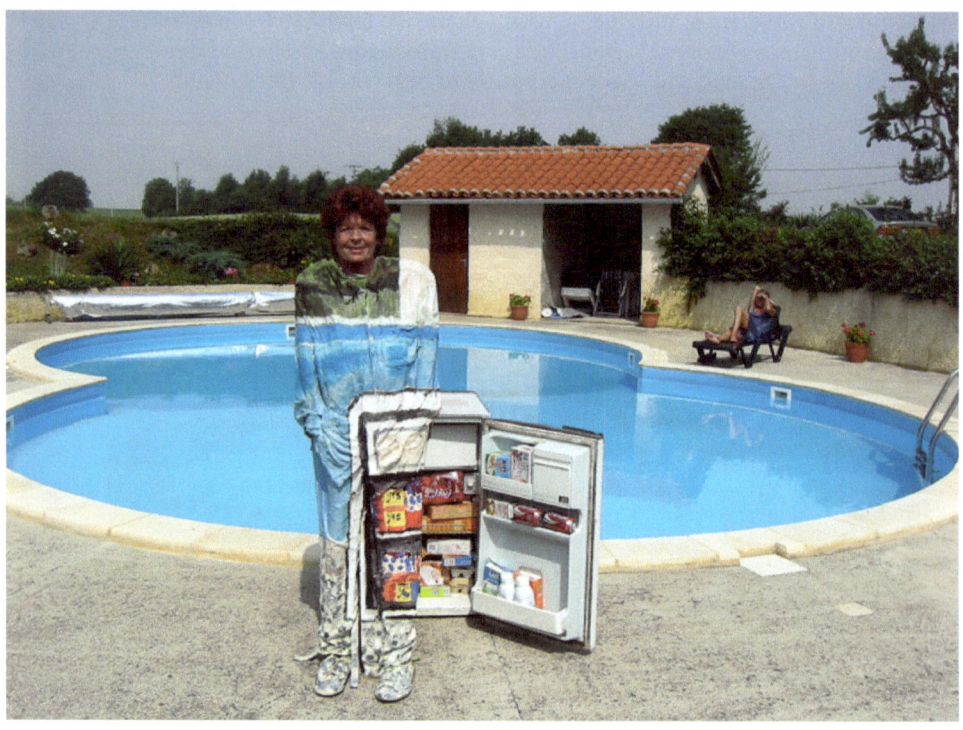

Swimming-pool, 2003 Pro-cryptic painting (acrylic on board and protective suit) color photograph, 75 x 50 cm

connecting elements in the swimming-pool series. The consternation in this case is caused by the mental incompatibility of the displayed items. The connecting elements are to be found in the swimming-pool and the household appliance both being owned by the camouflaged person, he being the beneficiary of the use of both. However, the refrigerator, considered to be a bare necessity and present in practically every household, is positioned in front of a pool, a pure luxury item with the exclusive task of serving as a status symbol and a source of pleasure/joy. It is this underlying contradiction that causes the onlooker to be startled.

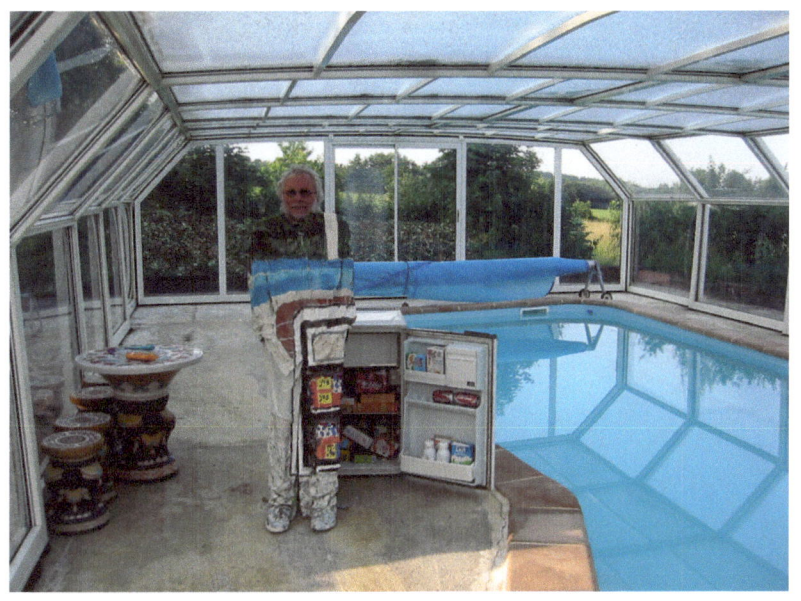

Swimming-pool, 2003 Pro-cryptic painting (acrylic on board and protective suit) color photograph, 75 x 50 cm

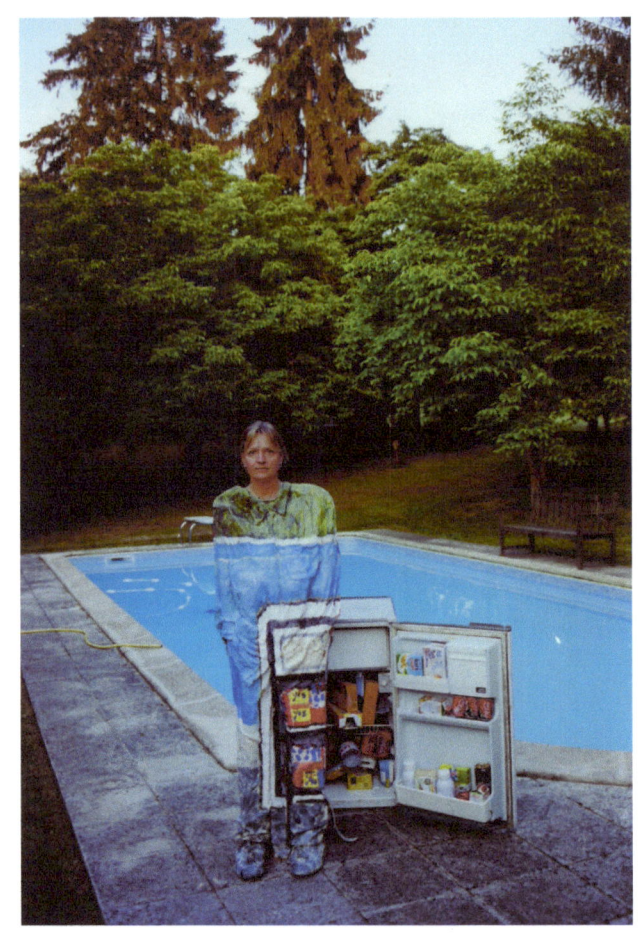

Swimming-pool, 2004 Pro-cryptic painting (acrylic on board and protective suit) color photograph, 75 x 50 cm

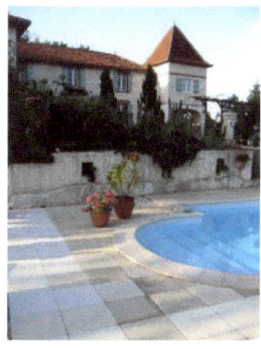 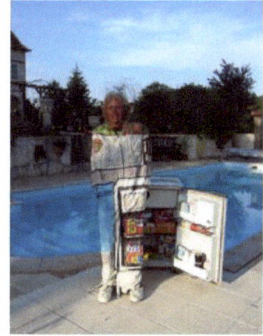 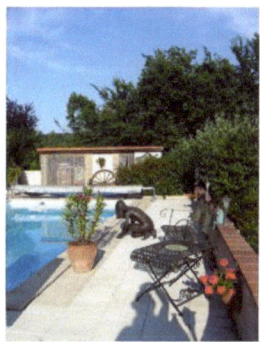

Swimming-pool, 2003 Pro-cryptic painting (acrylic on board and protective suit)
color photograph, 75 x 50 cm

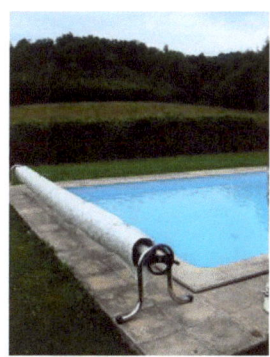 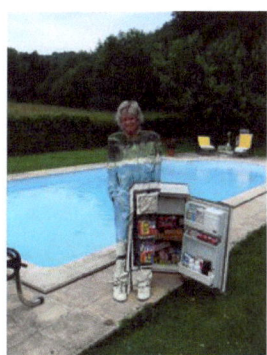 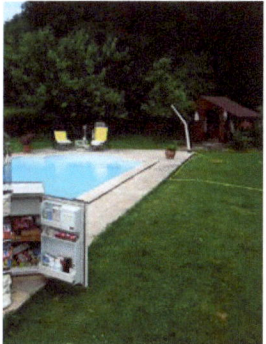

Swimming-pool, 2003 Pro-cryptic painting (acrylic on board and protective suit)
color photograph, 75 x 50 cm

High-gloss series

High-Gloss is a term that refers to a certain type of brilliant and shiny photography, shiny both as in the sense of shiny on the surface as in having a superficial content. This series of photographic installations has been envisioned as a simulation/ mimicry of landscape photographies.

Each photograph shows a panoramic landscape which incorporates a foreign and

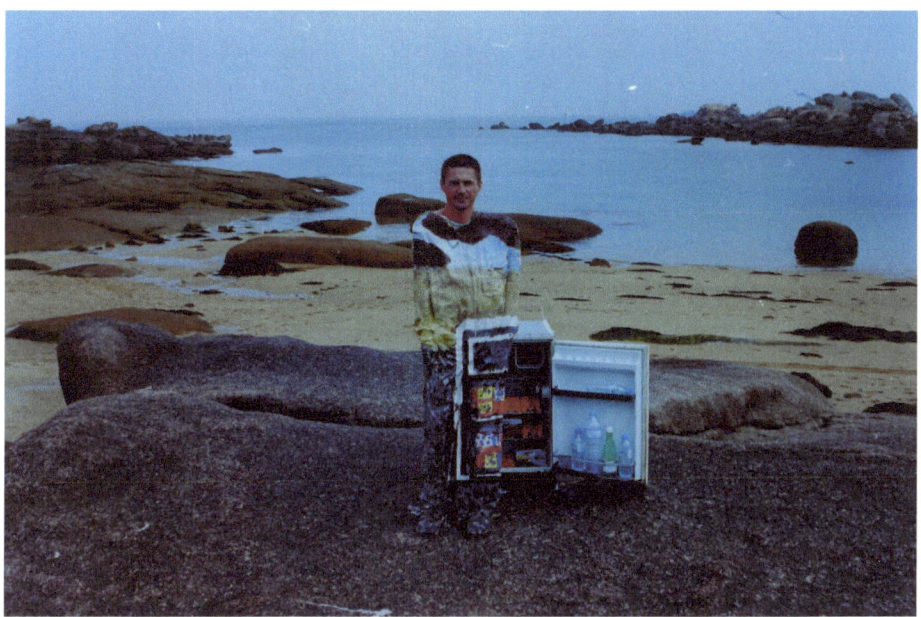

unexpected element with a somewhat startling effect on the onlooker. The merged human face is a relic and remains immovable while the rest of the body is camouflaged. What is traditionally displayed in this kind of high-gloss photography is changed in a 'revolutionary manner' by the presence of this remnant human element and it removes the evocative power of the landscape.

Untitled, 2002 Pro-cryptic painting (acrylic on board and protective suit) color photograph, 75 x 50 cm

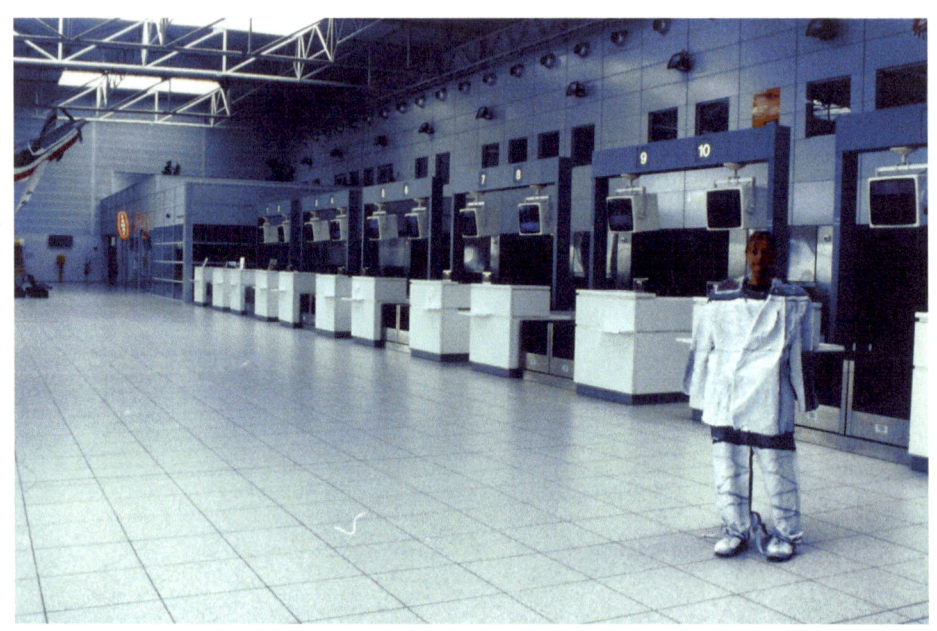

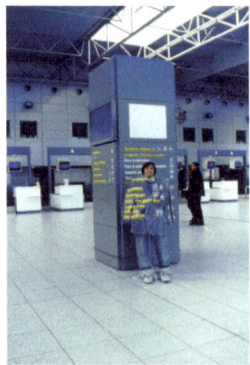

Untitled, 2002 Pro-cryptic painting (acrylic on board and protective suit) color photograph, 75 x 50 cm

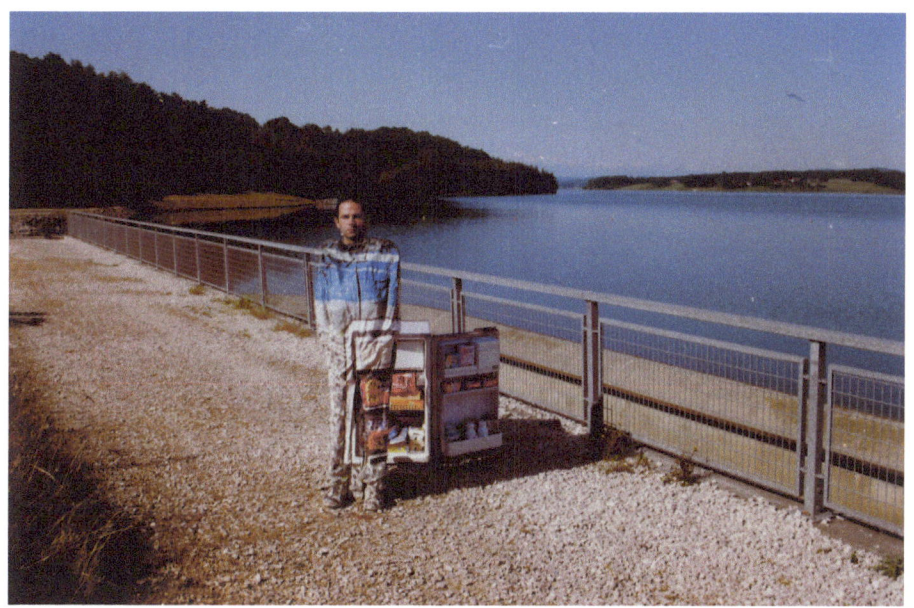

My work takes a critical approach to the way nature is being photographed and then commercialised as a blissful place.
Instead of having the presence of the artist devoted to the display of the beauty of the landscape scenery, the artist figure is made part of it. Consequently the artist introduces, through the means of camouflage, his own image into the natural Eden landscape leaving his face as a remnant part, thus visualising his narcissism. Disappearance of the individual subject...

Lake, 2004 Pro-cryptic painting (acrylic on board and protective suit) color photograph, 75 x 50 cm

My pastiche is like parody, it is the imitation of a peculiar or unique, idiosyncratic style (the so-called "Landscape Photography"). The wearing of an artistic mask (the fridge) serves as the neutral practice of mimicry.
My installations deal with the pastiche culture as a dialectical fragmentation of social life, where the norm itself is eclipsed, reduced to a proliferation of social codes.

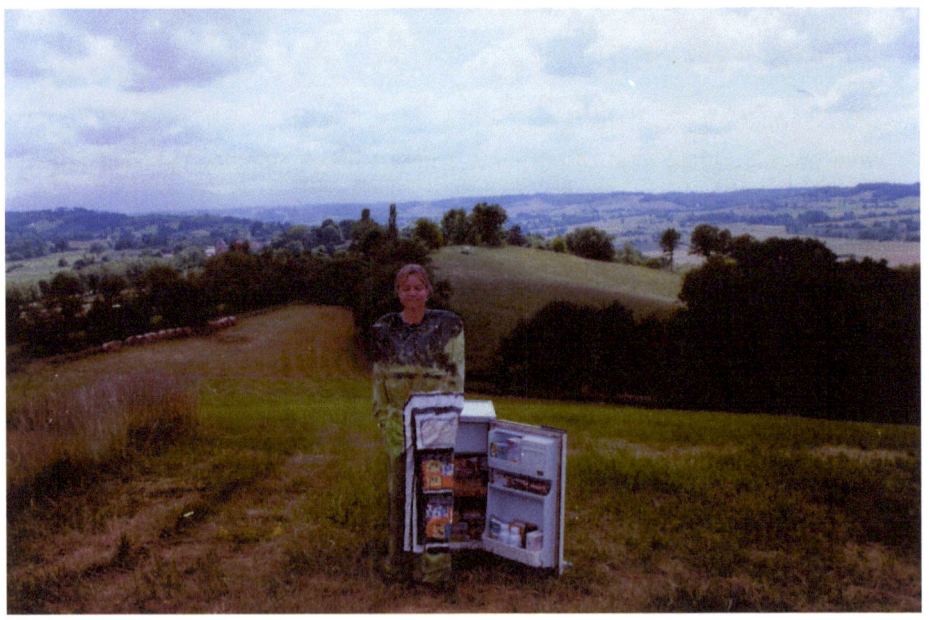

Untitled, 2002 Pro-cryptic painting (acrylic on board and protective suit) color photograph, 75 x 50 cm

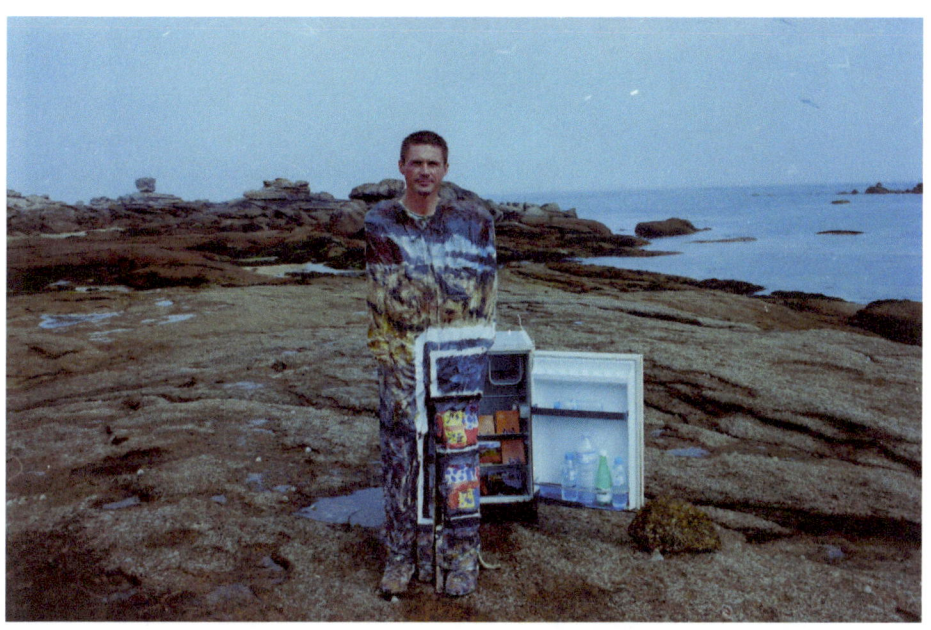

Untitled, 2004 Pro-cryptic painting (acrylic on board and protective suit) color photograph, 75 x 50 cm

In the High-Gloss series, the subject is dissolved and worked into a "simulacrum", constituting something like a mirage, a nuclear camouflage.

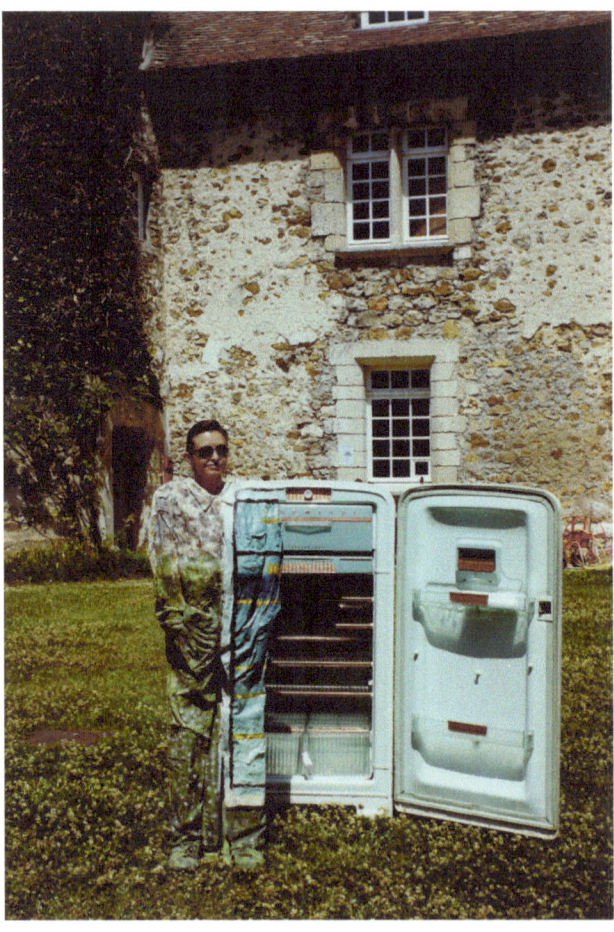

Untitled, 2003 Pro-cryptic painting (acrylic on board and protective suit) color photograph, 75 x 50 cm

Laurent La Gamba - Biography

Laurent La Gamba was born January 23, 1967 in Bondy, France. In 1982 he met Chloë Newton de Molina, whom he married in 1992.

Career

After studying at the Sorbonne in Paris (1993-98) and travelling abroad especially to Los Angeles, CA, USA, where he stays over long periods of time, he starts painting in the vein of the French *Figuration Libre* movement. His first show is held in Marsanne (Drôme-Provence,1999).

Laurent La Gamba sets up his studio in Monléon-Magoac (Hautes-Pyrénées) in 1995. His painting evolves hand in hand with photography: large canvases (using acrylic paint) which can be likened to American photorealism, he creates close-up portraits of his entourage, family and neighbours. In 2001, he undertakes a series of caustic self-portraits, where cigarette dangling from his mouth, his face painted in a photorealist fashion he morphs into a stewardess, a Mc Donald's manager, Bob the Builder or a veiled woman. The focus is on the face, the background and accessories are painted with haste. This series is completed with sme photo-montage work: a mixture of photography and painting (Tarbes Chamber of Commerce Show 2001). Excerpts of psychoanalyst Jacques Lacan's writings accompany his work. This combination tips La Gamba's oeuvre into conceptual photography. And thus begin the first in situ Camouflages and pro-cryptic installations which he works on whilst obtaining a Pollock-Krasner Foundation grant and being artist in residence at the La Napoule Art Foundation (Mandelieu, France 2001). He dresses his models or himself in white suits which are then painted into a chosen environment to have them then diasappear. At first there are indoor portraits and then more elaborate outdoor portraits/ camouflages in supermarkets, airports, in front of cars, fridges, cookers... From his corner of France called *Monléon Magnoac* he manages to lead a full artistic career in his native country and on an International level, especially in the United

States in museums and Contemporary Art Centers (several prizes in 2003 in San Diego, Helena, Winchester).

He also creates videos and installations. Recent shows in New York, Anchorage, Montréal, Taiwan (Juming Museum), Portland. His outlook on mankind is militant, on the edge of social critique.

— *Brianti, Sylvio (2010) (in French). Traces d'artistes: dictionnaire de l'art moderne et contemporain Édicité. ISBN 9782916650104.*

Public collections

- The San Diego Art Institute, San Diego, USA
- La Napoule Art Foundation, Mandelieu-La Napoule, France
- Art Center Waco, Waco, Texas, USA
- Arizona State University Art Museum Video Archives, Tempe, Arizona, USA
- The Space Museum, Toulouse, France
- CAMAC-Marnay Art Center, Marnay-sur-Seine, France
- L'imagerie, Lannion, France
- N.A.P., New Arts Program, Kutztown Museum, Pennsylvania, USA
- MoFA, Florida State University Museum of Fine Arts, Tallahassee, Florida. USA
- Griffin Museum of Photography, Winchester, USA

- Artothèque, Hennebont, France

- The Iowa Biennial Exhibition Research Archives, University of Iowa, USA

- MoMA / Franklin Furnace Artist Book Collection – Museum of Modern Art, NY, USA

- Juming Museum of Art, Taipei, Taiwan, R.O.C.

"Trained as a painter, French artist Laurent La Gamba likewise mingles absurdity and a seriousness of intent in a series of color photographs that rely on a performative aspect. The subject of each image is an individual wearing a costume painted to match a section of supermarket display - shelves of various brands of pet food, for example. Thus camouflaged, the figures are subsumed by namebrand identities, calling attention to the manner in which we define ourselves in a commodity-based consumer culture." *Kate Hackman, Focus on Photo, Society for Contemporary Photography shows extol substance, The Kansas City Star, Nov. 2002*

"In exploring the fundaments of camouflage, La Gamba reveals a means of protection from urban manifests. Like an animal, he blends with his milieu, bringing pulse to a humdrum world. In search of his hiding place, he creates painted installations for his static effigy. In doing so, he seeks the most profound realism, becoming a pragmatic episode of monotony. Ironically, within in the empty vacuum of repetition, his artificiality renders personification. Thanks to La Gamba, the face of a milk carton is forever changed. Rather than instigating nourishment, opening the fridge will now become the door to a mirror. In labels, lids and containers, La Gamba appears, his white coat tailored to suit. Yet within his pose lies a sense of mendacity, innate to the many masks stripping him of self. Insatiable, his contagion adheres to no limits, liberating the artist into an omnipresent being. As part of all seen or overlooked, he brings a new face to the everyday, with his stories wryly told. As a whole, he offers a critical or cynical view, raising curiosity within tedium. Some may call him quirky, others just plain odd, but in his idiosyncrasy, he creates a wave of colour, superseding daily rituals. Aside from effervescence, his work leaves a dismal residue. In his masquerade, La Gamba withdraws from the metropolis, guarded from conformity by his protective skin. This hedonistic artist shows no qualms, yet with his pet-like manner, becomes an emblem of domesticity." **Louise Thompson, Pro-cryptic Photography: Photography by Laurent La Gamba, Wilson Street Gallery Review, May 2003**

"For the artist, pro-crypsis is a rather technical term that he uses to describe the physical transformation of an entity in order to blend with its immediate environment. " I have been always been fascinated by the camouflage phenomenon. I was also looking for a term that could translate the French word "homochromie" which comprises this idea of "chromatic merging." Then, I came to this idea of defining my photographic art and installations as "Pro-cryptic Photography". And what about this recurring cigarette: "I think that the temptation of using the same cigarette each time can be seen under two lights: one, there is the will to play with this virtual element of identification (I don't smoke, therefore the viewer has not only no idea who I am, but also it means that I can create any idea of the artist's "image", and two, it echoes back to my self-portrait series in which I always use this cigarette as a pattern from one painting to the next."

[Photo ID: examining the figure through photography] Suzanne Opton/ Gwen Laine/Laurent La Gamba, MOCA, Museum of Contemporary Art, Fort Collins, U.S.A., curated Erica France.

Laurent La Gamba
The art of camouflage

Texts and illustrations collected by Claire Duane

Matisse 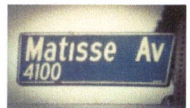 *Avenue Books*

ISBN: 9781500655211

Laurent La Gamba
The art of camouflage

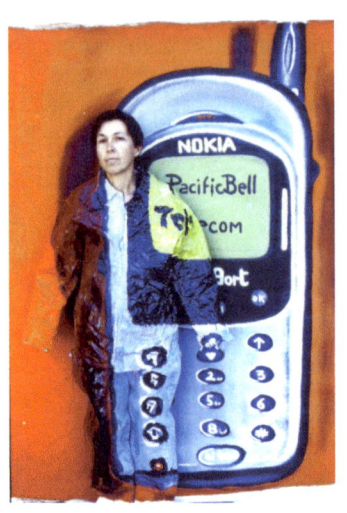

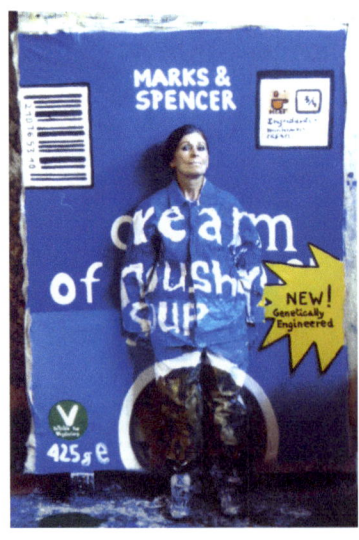

www.ingramcontent.com/pod-product-compliance
Lightning Source LLC
Chambersburg PA
CBHW040809200526
45159CB00022B/125